# The Microwave Way to Software Project Management

# The Microwave Way to Software Project Management

*Bas de Baar*

Writers Club Press
San Jose New York Lincoln Shanghai

**The Microwave Way to Software Project Management**



Writers Club Press
an imprint of iUniverse, Inc.

For information address:
iUniverse, Inc.
5220 S. 16th St., Suite 200
Lincoln, NE 68512
www.iuniverse.com

ISBN: 0-595-22711-2

Printed in the United States of America

*This one goes out to the one I love.*

# Contents

# Preface

Have you ever woken up thinking "how did I get here?" I'm not referring to not knowing where you are physically, but to the status of your project activities. One morning, you had a delay of your software project on your hands. Thinking back you know how it became late, as they always do, one day at a time. And the worst part is, you know how it could be avoided, or at least not escalate in the situation your in at that particular morning. You know it, but you didn't do it.

If you have woken up like that once or more, we share same experiences. I know what to do, I know best practices by heart. But sometimes it seems the heart is a long way from the brain. Attempts are made. More then once. But there is always that morning.

This book started out as my personal vendetta against all mornings waking up with trouble about a project. It originally appeared on the internet as a course on software project management at SoftwareProjects.org. Some people called it a "course", others a "guide". Whatever. While I wrote the content I kept one thing in mind: "if you have one day to talk about software project management, what would you tell?" I surely wouldn't be yapping about Great Graphs. This book is an upgraded version from the original internet publication at SoftwareProjects.org.

Doing software projects in organisations is a people-intensive process. The fears and wishes of stakeholders determine the path the project will follow. This book will tell the story of software project management from this point of view. It explains on how to handle the expectations of the stakeholders, and how he/she can use 'traditional techniques', like Gantt-charts, to manage the expectations. The book will provide the reader in a short period of time all the essential information on running a small to medium sized software project in real organisations.

Most of the content is common sense, everything is at least my personal experience. I guess if it works for me, it could also benefit other project managers. The approach of the book is straight forward: develop several principles one should stick to leading a project, explain how to use them on several project managers tasks during a project, and most of all, provide a way to put the techniques into practice (for those who quit smoking, you know how hard it is to break bad habits).

The title of this book is "The Microwave Way to Software Project Management". This is due to the fact that I wonder why most books on the management of software projects are so big and boring. It should be fast and fun: The Microwave Way!

The entire content of this book is written by me as an individual, based upon my own ideas and experiences, and are therefor my own opinions. There is no connection with any company what so ever.

## Audience

This is a book about software project management, so it is obviously intended for people who are managing software projects or have the ambition to do so in the near future. However, the less formal you are, the best suited this book is for you. I treat the subjects fast and I try to make the experience as entertaining as possible.

Experienced managers can use this book as a guide to a stakeholders-centred approach to software project management.

Students, or "project-managers-to-be" can use it as a crash course. It is written by some one who studied the concepts of project management methods, went to work as a project manager, and was totally confused between the differences of the methods and reality. The book provides the glue between the things one will see in the real world and the techniques that are available to software engineering and project management.

## Book overview

In this section an overview of the chapters in this book is provided. The first chapter provides the main principles a software project manager has to follow, the mindset he or she should have to lead a happy project. The remaining chapters are based around specific parts of this mindset, and provide insight into the specifics of the areas of concern.

### *Chapter 1: Mindset of the software project manager*

Since I saw on public television magic tricks revealed, saw someone explain how to slice a woman in half, David Copperfield bores me. Knowing how the magic works, will shatter your dream. As software projects take place in reality, dreaming is not an option, and therefor it's very profitable to know how the tricks of the stakeholders surrounding the project work (if you find this a weird twist in a sentence, wait until you read the rest).

Stakeholders are all the people involved in a project, the customer, the supplier, the boss, the user, you name it. As a project manager you have to deal with them; it's even worse, they will determine if your software project will be a success or a failure. This first chapter will describe an image a software project manager should have engraved in his mind. If you see it, you will surely recognise it. It's simple and short, so much easier to keep in your head then a huge binder with methods.

### *Chapter 2: Intake*

Ever got a present where you thought "what is this?" Ever got something from your superiors nicely rapped in a paper with in neon letters 'project' on it, where you thought "what?" Then this chapter is surely for you. Problems, ideas or just plain stupidity are quickly labelled 'project' and handed over to a project manager. The intake is to clarify what is meant.

### *Chapter 3: Requirements determination*

What ever you do, what ever you make, you should know what to do or to make. After an intake the global contours of the project are outlined by goals and scope. You should get more specific though. It's this getting more specific that requirements determination is all about.

### *Chapter 4: Requirements validation*

As a kid I played this little game at school we called 'telephone line'. Twenty kids were hurdled up into a circle. One started by whispering a sentence in the ear of his neighbour, so the other kids couldn't hear what was said. The neighbour would say the same sentence to his neighbour, and so on, until the sentence was 'round circle'. The fun of the game was comparing what the last one had heard with what was originally said. Mostly, they didn't even come close.

During the project the requirements stated at requirements determination should be validated. This validation goes two ways: are we meeting the requirements, and are the requirements still valid. This section handles the requirements made to the product part of the project.

### *Chapter 5: Project progress*

In Holland we have this huge (200km) ice-skating event, the "Elf Steden Tocht" which means "Eleven cities tour". On the course are several check points, which in fact are the eleven cities, where you have to get a stamp. Getting these stamps is very important. Actually, the race is about passing all the checkpoints.

In a project it's all about getting the approvals to keep on going. This section handles giving feedback on the requirements made to the process. Are we still within time and budget, and are the project constraints still the same?

*Chapter 6: Risk management*

I cannot tell you what the future will bring. No one can, although some people believe they can. This whole project thing is based upon assumptions and estimations, on guesses and hunches. Sometimes we are wrong. In a project we have to deal with this as a fact of life. Enter "risk management". A risk is the possibility of loss of some kind. It's all about what can be different from what we believe right now. Not just what can go wrong, but possibilities can arise also if the future brings not what you think it will. "Dealing with uncertainty" would be a good subtitle for this section.

*Chapter 7: The Bigger Picture*

This final chapter will cover two aspects of doing projects in a larger context, your organisation. The aspects are how to handle policies issued on what systems you may use, and how it should be constructed, and how you can introduce a "project approach" into an organisation in such a way, your own job as a project manager will be more effective.

## Sofi's Choice

Sometimes I wish the job of software project manager has more danger. Walking around, shooting from the hip at your opponent. Employees in fear, 'cause there's a new project manager in town. Something like that.

Sometimes I wish the job of software project manager is cool. In the 1995 movie "Hackers" actor Jonny Lee Miller is painting his laptop with camouflage colors. Cool. Mine is black, sadly.

But there *is* danger. It *is* cool. That's why being a software project manager is the choice of Sofi. Sofi is the new heroine we desperately need in our profession. It's like Lara Croft is kicking some programmer butt. You will meet a picture of Sofi at the start of each chapter. It's cool being a software project manager, 'cause it's also Sofi's choice!

Sofi

# Acknowledgements

Being Dutch has its disadvantages: I'm not a native English speaker, as you already might have guessed. A lot of people have contributed to make the text readable and understandable in the English language. I would especially like to thank Jessica Naish and Thomas Corcoran for their help.

Of course, grammar was not my only concern when writing the material for "The microwave way", the content was reviewed by several people to stop me from rambling on, and put some much needed structure in the text. I am in debt by the following people who proof read the manuscript and helped me with their constructive criticism: Matthijs Claessen, Rick Lefevere and Martijn Simons.

This book also introduces Sofi, the way cool software project manager who appears at the start of every chapter. These incredible images are created by Maarten Peerdeman. I am very grateful for his effort.

Finally, I would like to thank my wife, Simone, who supports me every day.

# Acknowledgements

# Chapter 1

## Mindset of the Software Project Manager

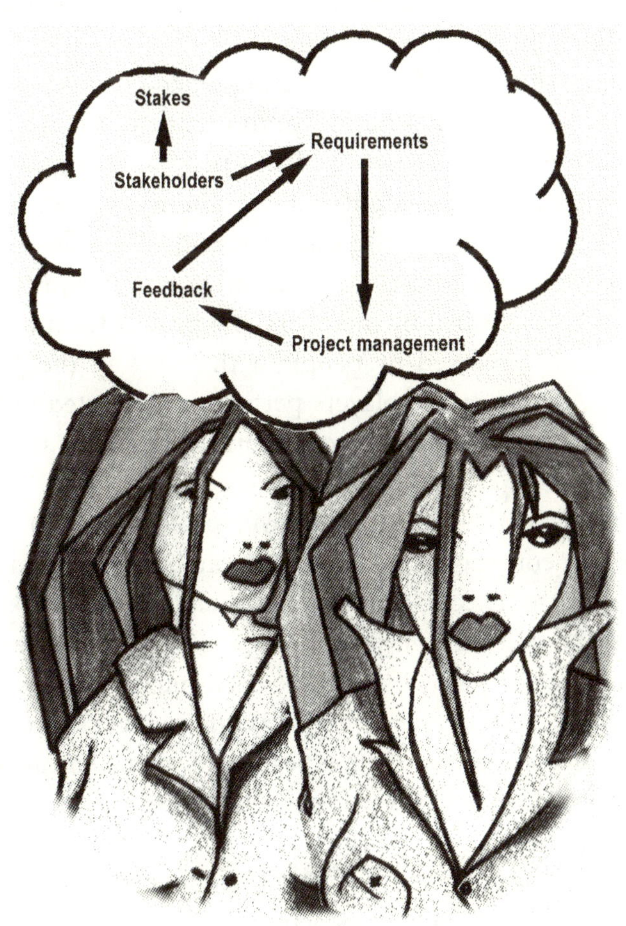

## 1.1. Staging the project for the stakeholders

The thrill of having tickets for the opening night for Andrew Lloyd Webber's new play on Broadway is in no comparison to the performance on amateurs night in our local town hall. Both are plays, both have players who conduct a series of lines to an audience. Prices differ, the quality of the players and props should give a serious gap in comparison. However, is there a difference in the appreciation of the audience? Is the night of those who went to Broadway more memorable then those who didn't cross our county line?

Most people would argue, it depends. It depends on the expectations of the audience. If they pay a bundle of money just to see some famous actor, they should be on Broadway. If it's people having fun in acting they want to see, amateurs night is surely the way to go. The staging should fit the expectations of the audience, and all is well.

A project has some aspects common to plays (not just tragedies). Some tricks are performed by members of a project team (the players) which are closely observed by people with stakes in the project, the stakeholders. As long as the players perform as expected by the audience, everybody is happy. The principles presented in this section aim at precisely that.

This book covers the subject of *software* projects. Any project which has a larger part concerning software in it, can be categorised as such.

You will be introduced to the central principle of this book: the "flow of the stakes"; a software project manager should *know the flow* and have it printed in his brain, it should be his mindset. It is a way to catch the expectations, to integrate all expectations of several people, and to make sure people know that their expectations are taken care of.

The main function of this section is to make you aware of this principle, to let you know there is a flow. It is not intended to provide a full depth analysis of every aspect of it. I try to do that in the other sections, but the true depth you can only view in practice.

*"A basic principle of Lao-tse's teaching was that this Way of the Universe could not be adequately described in words, and that it would be insulting both to its unlimited powers and to the intelligent human mind to attempt to do so."* [Hoff, 1982]

It is perhaps a little much, but it gives you a certain idea; well, any way, see the flow as the apotheosis of this chapter, first we build up some context.

## 1.2. Software project managers' problem

For long, the art of the management of a software project is really an art, it's a trick that's difficult to master. The difficulty lies in the central problem the software project manager is faced with; appropriately named 'the software project managers' problem' [Boehm, 1989].

Everyone effected by the project, direct or indirect, has something to say, again direct or indirect, and will do so. Everyone wants to get the best from this project for him personally, or for his (part of the) organisation. It's the job of the software project manager to see that everyone gets what he wants, in one way or another. He has to "make everyone a winner" [Boehm, 1989].

In this respect, the role of the project manager becomes that of a negotiator. The customer always wants to have it all for free, the user wants to have to greatest functionality, the programmer doesn't want to document, but wants to use the coolest compilers. The software project manager has to make them all happy.

## 1.3. Focus on the stakeholders

The entire process of software projects is strongly stakeholder-driven. It's their wishes, fears, dreams, their *stakes* (hence the name) that determine the course of the projects. A *stakeholder* can be a project team member, an employee of the user organisation, or a senior manager. Virtually, it can be anyone, as long as they have something to do with the project.

The stakes are the crown jewels of the holders. They stick to them, they defend them, they are married to them. They also make up the words to formulate their expectations. The individuals will take all actions necessary to defend their stakes, or to get near the realisation of them.

Stakes can be in two directions: *fears* or *wishes*. With the first there is a stake to lose, with the second there is something to gain. Either way, stakes are sacred things; anyone, including a project manager, should not try to mess with them.

Again, in order to do anything with the stakes of the holders, the project manager should be the greatest negotiator he possibly can be.

## 1.4. Indirect communication of stakes

The human nature is not always direct. So, it's not always clear what the stakes are. Sometimes stakeholders communicate them directly, most of the time they don't. The level of communication is indirect; stakes are contained in *requirements* made to the project, *process and products*. Requirements are always a clearly defined state that is desired. This is in contrast with stakes, which are generally vague and abstractly formulated (if formulated at all).

An oversimplified example: a stake of a programmer is "to be also involved in way cool new technologies like my brother-in-law", say Java; the corresponding requirement could be that "the system can only be programmed in Java". The requirement can be stated surrounded by other technical arguments, but it's only the stake mentioned that caused it to appear.

So, the project manager has this project, surrounded by requirements he has to take care of. But, remind yourself, they are *not* the stakes, they are *not* the crown jewels you may not touch. So you can mess with the requirements? Can you?

## 1.5. What's it worth?

Sounds simple, however, getting the requirements is one, finding out their corresponding stakes is another. Why bother anyway, what is it worth? A lot. As mentioned earlier, one can't effectively change the stakes, but one can change the requirements as long as they keep on supporting the stakes. In this way there is room to negotiate a set of requirements to the project, which do not conflict, match the stakes and thus making every one a winner! Right?

Taking it one step back. A stakeholder formulates a requirement for the software project. E.g. senior management states that "the project should be finished before the end of August." The project manager has to deal with it. When this deadline is no problem, he can rest assure. However, it's a software project, so the deadline will be a problem. The way to handle it is to get some information on the stakes that caused to formulate this requirement. Perhaps it's the old "don't want to loose my face when my projects get delayed." That being the case, the project manager can offer alternatives that don't violate the stake, like keeping the deadline, but postpone a subsystem. Changes are that alternative requirements that keep supporting stakes, are accepted. Maybe not easily, but a project manager should do something to earn it's money.

An example, taken from Brooks [1995]:

"*...the reluctance to document designs is not due merely to laziness or time pressure. Instead it comes from the designer's reluctance to commit himself to the defence of decisions which he knows to be tentative. 'By documenting a design, the designer exposes himself to the criticisms of everyone, and must be able to defend everything he writes. If the organisational structure is threatening in anyway, nothing is going to be documented until it's completely defensible.'*"

## 1.6. Stakeholders during the project

The first influence of the stakeholders on the project is usually the most influential. And it's at the start of the project. The demands and constraints issued on the process and the products they produce sets the stage for the entire duration of the software project. The primary task of the project managers should be to reassure the stakeholders that their stakes are taken care of, that what they said, is heard. For the entire project the project managers task consists of giving the feedback to the stakeholders of the state their requirements are in.

Feedback could take the following form:

- Tests
- Test results
- Prototypes
- Reports
- Evaluations
- Plans
- Benchmarks

This part is essential, but easily forgotten. If the project manager does not keep giving feedback, the slightest hint (or rumour) of not sticking to the stakes, may set a stakeholder on the war path against the once so happy project.

## 1.7. Flow of the stakes

Having said all this, where does it leave the software project manager? In order to have a "happy project" a software project manager should respect the flow of the stakes, as illustrated in the diagram below, and must ensure that stakes go "full cycle".

Uhhr, well, let's describe this "flow" in a few steps:

- Stakeholders have stakes

- Stakeholders communicate their stakes by means of requirements to the process or the product
- Project management should make every stakeholder a winner by accepting and inventing requirements that keep satisfying the stakes of individual stakeholders and are not conflicting with the general process and product
- Project management should give continuos feedback on the state of the stakes
- Based upon the feedback, the *requirements* might change. In this way, a new cycle starts.

**You must know this flow!**

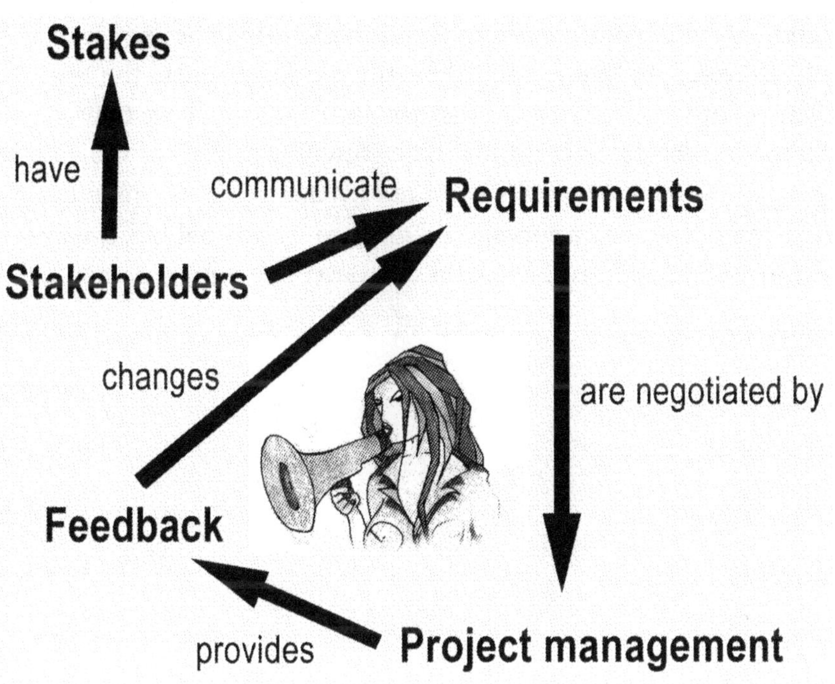

## 1.8. That's all folks!

So, now you know the flow. For the coming days, try to fit all that surrounds you into this flow, view the world through these glasses. As you already might have guessed the concepts behind The Flow are not limited to software projects.

The principles on how to invent win-win conditions are discussed in general books like "Getting to yes" [Fisher and Ury, 1983]. They even mention its use in hostage situations. The indirect communication of stakes can even be viewed in "Men are from Mars, women are from Venus" [Gray, 1992]. If a girl states to her boy-friend "I want you to listen to my problem" (requirement to the process) the stake of the girl typically would be the reduction of her stress by talking on the subject, the boys' typical interpretation of her stake would be "she wants the problem fixed." To know exactly how this works, just read the book.

The point I want to make is that you don't actually have to work currently in a software project to try The Flow. Try to view as much of life as possible with your glasses coloured by the concepts presented. I'm not claiming these concepts should guide your normal life, it is just an exercise! This is still just a book on software project management.

# Chapter 2

## *Intake*

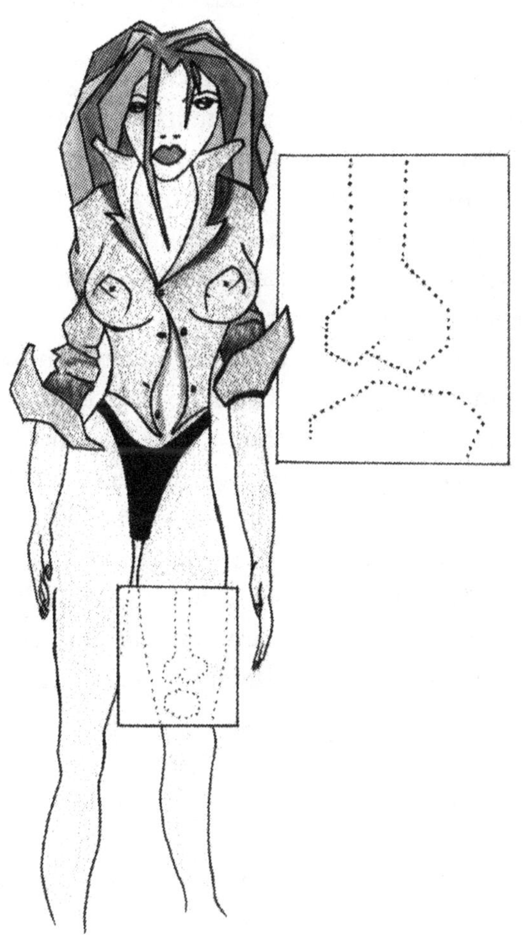

## 2.1. Introducing the intake

Movies are great. Women get pregnant and 5 minutes later their kid goes to college. One moment the family has the need for a vacation, the next shot they're floating on the canals of Amsterdam. And that's all just swell. Not many people want to view the hours of discussions around the kitchen table on deciding what country to go to. Not many people want to see every moment of a woman in labour, and watching the growing pains of a teenage kid, for hours and hours. Living a movie is great, you can skip the boring parts.

Being in the highest ranks of management is great. One moment you're in a wooden cabin in the mountains together with your fellow priests reflecting the need for the strategic development of a new product line. The next moment you're reviewing the results after taxes the new product line brings in. Life is good being at the top.

Meanwhile back in the jungle of middle management, lesser gods are struggling to pick up a vague comment made up in a wooden cabin up in the mountains, make something of it, and turn it into reality. Being a software project manager you meet strange objects thrown toward you from above. It could be no more then a little statement, or it can be a complete part of an organisation coping with the remains of old mission impossible. The thing they have in common though is their label: *project.*

If you're a permanent member of the organisation, you're just new, or you're from a third party supplier, the moment a software project manager comes into the picture, there is already something labelled as project. The 'chicken-or-egg-first'-dilemma does not apply to project management; first is the project, secondly the project manager. Sadly. The first task of the software project manager is to reengineer the situation that led to the project. The stakes of the people who initiated the activities now labelled as project should be clear. The requirements resulting from that should be known. These are the tasks during the *intake* of the project.

All may not be crystal clear. Time schedules may already be stated, without any one knowing what should be done in the first place. Goals can be formulated with such an ambiguity that anything produced satisfies the goal. The sad part of it is that stakeholders have already formulated their requirements. They may not have communicated them, but in their minds expectations are already in a particular direction. You should sort it out. It's a dirty job, but someone's got to do it.

At the end of the intake the project manager has aligned the project in such a way that he/she is willing to take the commitment for it, or he/she found out it is impossible and gives the job back (Yes, you have that choice!).

## 2.2. For all the right reasons

Doing projects is hip. At least, that's the impression one might get given the number of projects and project managers around. It's not that surprising when you keep in mind that our ever changing world asks for activities with ever increasing complexity. We have to keep reinventing the way we do things. Invent it, and then throw it away, because of it's obsolescence; what works one time, has no use a second time. It's the environment where projects survive as the fittest.

A project, by definition, is a temporary activity with a starting date, specific goals and conditions, defined responsibilities, a budget, a planning, a fixed end date and multiple parties involved. You know what you have to do, do it, once, and that's the end of it. That's a project. However, being hip has it's disadvantages. Our local housing office has a permanent project manager for financial controlling. This is a on going activity for the office, and the project manager does it as his full time, never ending job. What ever he's managing, it surely ain't a project.

There is no real harm in naming a tiger an elephant or vice versa. No one gets hurt by naming his job a project, even if it doesn't fit the definition by a mile. But don't be surprised if techniques for projects don't work on 'projects-just-by-name'. Don't be amazed when applying the techniques may seem like killing a bumble-bee with a machine gun. Don't get mad when other people don't know why you're doing an easy job the hard way, by making a project out of it.

Start a project, but only for the right reasons. Not for the heck if it. Not because of the cool acronym. Or the status.

Look for the following aspects:

- Starting date
- Specific goals and conditions
- Defined responsibilities
- A budget
- A planning
- A fixed end date
- Parties involved

And then, if it looks like a duck, walks like a duck and quacks like a duck, it probably is a duck. However, if it doesn't come close, raising the question of treating it like a project is the right thing to do. There may be an easier and much simpler solution.

*"Often (...) top management has no project; it merely has a problem and does not know how to, or does not want to, find a solution. So, it expects the players to find the way. Much social and industrial unrest can be caused by top management not having real projects, but only having the desire to get rid of a problem."* [D'Herbemont and César, 1998]

If you don't find all the aspects named above at this moment in time, it is possible. Wait, and make the final judgement at the end of the intake. Working on one of the subjects, might cause one of the aspects to popup.

## 2.3. Determine cause and goal

There is a meaning to life. If you have a religious or scientific point of view, there is a way we're all going. There's some purpose to what we do. And that's nice. The days that we did something just because someone told us to do so, are over, I hope.

All activities should have a goal they support. And, even better, a goal that is seen as useful and achievable. Digging a hole, so another poor fool can fill it again, is a goal, but fails the other criteria. You may laugh at this, and wave it away as trivia and as a far stretch from reality. You poor soul, you are probably not long out of reality back here in the asylum.

Projects, being a collection of activities, have goals. They should be the answer to every 'why'-question about the project. Reviewing several projects, you will probably find some statements about the goals to be achieved. I'm sure searching information about the cause of the project however, will give you less data. And it's the cause that provides you with some hint about the usefulness of the goals. It can give insight on dependencies with other projects; so you can avoid another project filling the hole you just dug.

The following questions may give you a start in your search for the answer on the big WHY:

- What strategic decision lead to this project?
- How does this project relate to the business plan?
- Is this project the follow up of another project?
- What will be done with the results of this project?
- What will happen if this project doesn't happen?
- Is this project related to other projects that take place in the same time frame?
- Does the competition address the same issues taken on by this project?
- Why was such a project not performed earlier?

## 2.4. Determine stage

Think about your project as a Shakespearean tragedy. See it as a play with all your stakeholders on a stage, wearing tights, big floppy hats and all talking in this weird language, "Wilt thou be gone? It is not yet near day." It helps you to put things into perspective, and it will not be far from reality.

During the project intake the software project manager should create a picture of who the stakeholders are. Before the play can start, you should at least know your cast. D'Herbemont and César [1998] call it "the field of play":

*"In theory, nothing is simpler than to draw up the field of play for a project. It defines itself. (...) A new information system is to be introduced? The players are the computer suppliers and the users. (...) However, defining the field of play always throws up surprises. One starts by working very calmly on a clean sheet of paper on a flip-chart. Soon there are ten sheets stuck to the wall on the meeting room, each filled with arrows, crosses and question marks. At the end of the day, there are still unanswered questions."*

So, basically what you do, is stand in front of a white board and start drawing relations between parties and people, indicating why they are a stakeholder in the project.

The field of play consists of groups and individuals. However, when we talk about demands, only individuals should be considered. When it seems a group makes any demands, or indicates other kind of properties normally associated with individuals, one has to look for a leader of the group, a representative, and substitute this person for "the group". It is not a group that has dreams or wishes, it is a person.

In this way you also avoid assigning stakes to people based upon an assumption related to the group. This kind of "stereotyping" can cause bad decisions of the project management; what is seen as a win-win situation, may be regarded by the individual as a complete disaster.

## 2.5. Determine constraints

We Dutch are cheap, or at least, that is what's suggested. In Belgium they claim that the Dutch are buried face downwards to have more slots to park our bicycles. I think you can say that we try to avoid spending too much money. If you would do a software project here in the Netherlands you would see a very strong tendency to save as much money as possible. However, never heard of a place where there is an unlimited budget.

My cheapness (being Dutch) is an illustration for the more earthier matters concerning a project: trying to get a fix on the limited stuff you need to proceed to the more noble cause of building a system. Whatever you have to create, whatever the cause of the project may be, there will always be *constraints* set to the project. These conditions determine the space in which the project organisation may operate. Therefore, you might think of this section of the book as the '*party pooper segment*'; they spoil the fun.

Project constraints consist of the following elements:

- *Money*: what's the project's budget? How is it constructed? Is everything fixed price or variable?
- *Time*: what is the time frame in with every activity should take place?
- *People*: which people are available for the project? What are their qualifications?

Constraints are not independent from each other. Using more people will cost you more money. If you want to use less time, you need more people (later on in this chapter we will see that adding more women to give birth to one child does not shorten the nine month period; this is rocket science project management). The point I'm trying to make is that *constraints are interdependent*.

A classic way to show this dependence is the use of the Project Constraints Triangle (I have no idea how the thing is really called). Imagine a 3-D space, where the x-axes represents the amount of people, the y-axes the amount of time and the z-axes the amount of money for the project.

The project is represented by a triangle within this 3-D space. The size of a project is displayed as the square of the triangle. The size is determined by complexity and the amount of the product to realise, and the desired quality.

A project with a constant size can have altering constraints. However, altering one constraint has influences on the others, because the square of the triangle stays the same.

The constraints are reflections of the stakes of the customer. However bold the constraints are stated by the customer, keep in mind they are requirements, not stakes, so there is room for some negotiation. Playing with the aspects of the project triangle (including size) may also satisfy the stakes of the customer, and therefore being accepted.

It seems that every customer wants the best product tomorrow, and it may not cost a penny. I'm sure these customers do exist. However, most top managers have a more realistic view of the matter. They know constraints must leave some room to operate. This doesn't mean they tell you.

## 2.6. Determine constraints–money

Money is the universal language. Or is it sex? I always mix 'em up…. Sex on a project can get you in jail, so I stick for the moment with 'money'. Everybody can relate to an amount of dollars. Function points, lines of code (LOC) or mean error deviations on mantissa buffer overflows (MEDOMBO, yep, made this one up) may mean nothing to people; but money talks!

This is probably why stakeholders around a project put such a big emphasis on this subject. It is finally a language they can understand. The great thing is, most items can be expressed in money. So, money is truly the universal language.

During the actual running of the project, the project manager should watch that not more money is spent, then is given to the project, and he should create nice graphs to see how the projects' balance sheet looks like. Duh! Perhaps, we will spend some time on this subject later, perhaps not.

At this moment, when the project is not actually started yet, or hardly, we can consider the schizophrenic situation where money talks heavily, and the thing to construct is not specified (this will be done during requirements determination). This is more a conversation between a dad and his son, where the son is going to buy a car...

Son: "It must cost at least $ 50.000,-."
Father: "You must have a car in the range of $25 till 30 thousand."
(I have no idea what a car costs in the US)

Neither of them said something of a little red Corvette or a little Purple Pinto. But they express their stakes directly into a metric, which they can compare. Dad has been ripped off before by his daughter with her car, and promised his wife that he wouldn't make the same mistake again, but he wants to pay some. Son just wants to cruise for babes, and assumes daddy is picking up the tab. So, if you were a negotiator on this one, forget the absolute amounts, and focus and learn from the stakes.

If, for example, a system has to be built for a customer, where the specification for it is 4 lines, and the customer wants it for not more then $ 10.000,-, the origin of this '10.000' would be the most valuable information a software project manager could get from this statement.

- The previous project that the financial controller handled, was originally estimated for $10.000 and went way over budget.
- There is a procedure which allows a certain level of management to make investments until $9.999, and for higher amounts one has to be a level up in the hierarchy.
- Five years ago the company asked for a quote on a completely different kind of system which was $20.000 and the brother of the nephew of the vice president said that this system was half the complexity of the other one.

By knowing the reasons you can deal with the amount. E.g. in the first case you can talk about a good way of tracing and tracking of the budget with the controller to avoid an unexpected overrun. Be creative.

A great source of information is the way a deal is either constructed, or how the customer (can also be an internal customer) wants the costs to be constructed: *fixed price* or *time-and-material* (T&M) based. In the first case, an exact amount is determined to deliver a certain good or service. In the second, the cost depends on the time and material actually spent, and will therefore be calculated after the job is done.

With fixed price, you really have to be sure you exactly know what you want as a good or service. Otherwise, you know exactly in advance what you have to pay for a system you don't need. With time-and-material you must be able to manage the project in such a way, that it really ends and doesn't drag on for years and years. If you view statements about the construction of the cost in this light, you get more and more insight in the truth (it really is out there, you know).

To summarise, in relation to the 'money' aspect, you have to answer the following questions:

- Which financial statements are already made in respect to the project?
- Who made these statements?
- Why did they make these statements (stakes)?
- Are there already statements on cost structure (fixed price vs. T&M)?
- If yes, why are these statements made (stakes)?
- How can you satisfy these stakes in such a way that there will be some room created to change absolute amounts?

Note on the last question: creating some room does not mean that you are actually going to change the amounts. The goal is to provide yourself with enough room to operate.

## 2.7. Determine constraints–time

"*The bearing of a child takes nine months, no matter how many women are assigned.*" [Brooks, 1995]. This is one of the most insightful observations made in the last 25 years on the subject of project management. It originates from 1975, and is written by Frederick Brooks in his article "The Mythical Man-Month". Welcome to the age of rocket science…

In the communication on the timing aspects of a software project, many mistakes are caused by the use of the unit man-month. Like the word says, it indicates actually "a month spent by one person". To determine the cost of the project, it is a fairly good unit: building the darn thing takes 3 man-months. You know what a guy costs per month, so you can do the math. But while the time passes, this statement will be shortened into "three months", either in written word, or in the minds of the people involved.

"How long does the project take?" "Oh, 3 months."

And then the fun starts.

"We need to finish the project sooner." "We'll add a resource. Problem fixed."

The problem with this kind of reasoning is the fact that some tasks cannot be split. Because of sequential dependence, or just because it is not possible (like the birth-thing). The trick is, that a man-month is an indicator for cost, and *not* for *progress*. So, while looking and discussing on time, be aware of this communication trap.

This may be the most valuable lesson, but it is not the only thing to consider about time at this moment. At this stage a detailed planning will not be created (luckily), but a global time-frame, with start-and end-date will surely be available, at least in the minds of the stakeholders concerned. Here holds the same thing as discussed in the 'money' paragraph: try to get a fix on 'why' these dates are chosen.

"It should then be finished because…"

- the most important manager takes a holiday (paid in advance) afterwards
- another project will start directly after it, and people are already allocated for this
- someone just yelled this date one day, and everybody uses the same mantra ever since

See if the deadline stated holds with the cause and target for this project.

You may perhaps miss something about planning and estimating stuff, this will be treated after the requirements are known (chapter "Project progress"). However, at this point in time some statements will be made about time, money and effort. If you have to rely on the input of experts for this (programmers, analysts), the best, and only thing you can do, is to talk to them and get an estimate

While doing this, focus on *why* they think this particular amount, is it similar to what they have done in the past, change some of the stuff you tell them, to see how that changes their behaviour. But most of all, listen seriously to them, let it be *their* estimation. Otherwise, if you have to work with the people later on in the project, and *you* provided the estimate, they normally will not agree and will not feel committed to do the work in *your* estimated time.

## 2.8. Determine scope

They decided to make no fuss about the wedding. A very small event for a few special friends. After a visit to her mother it was two small events, one wedding at city hall, one at the local church. When they left his mother, all old aunts were invited, and, all being of high age, would of course stay the night. The day she spoke with her best friend, so had to have this great dress, which would need three bridesmaids to carry the thing…

Sounds familiar? You don't have to plan a wedding to see something so elegant and easy, grow and grow and end up getting completely out of hand. You probably heard stories of people wanting to fix a dripping shower and ending up with a complete revision of their bathroom. You must know where to stop and then just simply stop.

With a software project it is essential to know the borders up front. Which aspects are allowed, which ones are off limits? If the goal is to cut cost, you can just fire every one. One could image that these kind of changes in personnel are not within the scope of a project. However, switching to a different technology would be. You are allowed to change internal procedure, but not the interfaces with external parties. "The Scope" can contain all kinds of statements. The trick is to get it as detailed as possible already at this stage. Together with the goal and constraints it provides information of the room to move.

The scope can be too large to fit in a certain time frame. The scope can be too small to satisfy the goal. In determining the scope you talk with parties concerned and ask two types of questions:

- Can we change this?
- Must we change this?

You should use the stuff you can change but not have to change, as ammunition to get the needed win-win situations, to be able to change the stuff you must. Wow, play this sentence again, Sam.

Suppose you are allowed to change the scope of training sessions, but you don't have to. Suppose you must change the way a certain department works, administrative procedures now done manually should be highly automated. Employees might become reluctant to become just a typing goat. By providing extra training that makes the employees more state-of-the-art in their field, and focusing on the fact that the time saved by the new system will be used to let them handle the more "challenging" cases, might create the win-win situation you need.

In this way, you should hammer a scope that fits the goals, constraints and expectations of the stakeholders. To avoid your aunts visiting, send them a piece of the wedding cake instead!

## 2.9. History

Psychotherapy tells you what you already knew: all your current problems are the result of your troubled childhood. You are now harassing your employees, because in high school the popular boys always bullied you. Your children wonder why you always provide them these trivial and obvious advises (actually, this is their problem, not yours). For the answer they should ask grandma how she succeeded so perfectly with her brainwashing their father/mother. You see, current problems find their origin in history.

By now, you know that I will make the bridge to software projects at this moment…so, yes, the same holds for software projects. This financial geezer sits on top of the budget (current problem) because the last project he controlled went way over the price (history). When we later on handle the subject of requirements determination you will see that most requests from users are caused by problems in their current systems. If they keep on emphasising that new billing-system X should perform check Y, you can bet your money on it in their current situation the lack of check Y is causing them a lot of extra work.

You could ask every stakeholder "Where were you on the night of…?", but something tells me this kind of McCarthyism is not beneficial for your start at the project. The most effective way is to have an informal talk with a senior and relaxed employee of the firm, who knows most of the important stakeholders and has been around in the organisation. Talk about the financial people, the bosses, the maintainers, the user groups and especially their managers. Where do they come from? Were they around last time a project was conducted? How did that come out?

Another way to get some taste of the history is to review old documents. Project plans, evaluations, strategic memo's, everything that is available and is somehow related, could be of use to build a view on the past.

Of course, if you are the senior and relaxed geezer of the organisation, you already know its history. In this case, just refresh clearly your memory.

## 2.10. Determine project strategy

By now you should have an idea about

- what the goal and reason of the project should be;
- who's involved in the project, direct or indirect;
- within which constraints you have to operate;
- what you can and must alter, and
- some background to anticipate current behaviour.

The next step is to determine what *strategy* the project should take. What kind of steps? In which sequence? With who? I'm not talking about a fully detailed description; "George will walk to the bathroom. George will take his trousers down." I'm talking about real strategy!

The 'traditional' steps within a software project are something like:

- we think about the subject
- we specify a solution for the subject
- we implement the subject
- we activate the subject in the organisation.

In project management lingua we call these steps *'phases'* and have cool names for them like 'analysis', 'specification', 'implementation', 'roll-out'.

At this moment you have to determine the 'phases', or mayor steps, you will take. A strategy would be to follow the steps as mentioned above (the 'traditional' one). You could do this, if what has to be done is absolutely clear and everyone agrees. If not, this is not the way to go. By the time you want to implement the stuff, what has been written in the specification is not valid any more, the people changed their minds. Because this is often the case, more common is a strategy where these steps (or some of them) are repeated several times. So, for example, instead of thinking for 6 months about a subject, and specifying a year, the project will go through several steps of 2 weeks thinking, 4 weeks specifying, etc. With every reiteration the specification gets more and more detailed, and you would benefit from the results of later steps.

The project strategy, like any other strategy, should be simple and logical; you must be able to explain it to someone not related to the project in 2 minutes. So, don't go rushing into methods and the technical talk, like incremental, spiral, tornado, waterfall, it is only camouflage for when you have no idea what your talking about.

If the goal is very unclear, the scope is totally undefined, the strategy would be to

- first get the goal clear,
- determine the scope,

- adjust the project according to the outcome of the previous step,
- execute the remainder of the project.

It's ok to have the later steps more general then the first ones. It is a very simple strategy, but you can explain it to everyone, and it makes sense. If you don't know exactly what to do, you first try to get that clear.

The strategy should be a result of all the information about the stakeholders you have collected. Consider the following situation. A chief of some users has a formal role in determining the requirements for the product. You, and some other people, fear that these requirements will go beyond the scope of the project. Intervening continuously with the user chief, may be considered as a threat to his independence or formal status. By creating some periodical steps to review the requirements in relation to the scope with stakeholders concerned, this problem can be overcome and result in the needed win-win situation. The decision of having these review steps for this case, is also an important part in determining the project strategy.

## 2.11. Determine project organisation structure

Darwin's natural selection is a great thing. The shape of every species is crafted over thousands of years, to get the functions it needs to survive in the environment it operates. If it does not have the necessary skills, it just dies and is doomed with extinction. All the beautiful, blonde, long legged creatures survive.

The Homo Projectus is an ugly thing. It survives in extreme situations, where dirt has to be shoved. In this case it has the aspects of a hog. But to get the right features to have a party of hogs operating in such a way the pack will survive, is something completely different. We cannot wait until nature has killed all unsuccessful project organisations (the hog party), so the software project manager has to help nature a little bit, tinkering with the organisation, so it might have a chance to survive in the corporate jungle.

A project organisation is a temporary thing. It will only exist from the projects start until its end. All the project team members are coming from different organisations or part of the organisation. They will all have a temporary assignment to the project. So, they have not only a project boss (the project manager, that might be you), but also their 'normal' boss, who orders him around when the employee is not in the project. These 'normal bosses' are an important group of stakeholders.

The project organisation should be a result from the project strategy, it should be constructed in such a way that the strategy can be implemented within the environment of the project ("look what the dog brought in, a presumptuous sentence"). A very obvious example: if the strategy contains an aspect of having independent reviews, the organisation should support its independence, by creating a separate working group with no ties to the other team members, e.g. But, I'm a little too far now mentioning working groups and the like.

The project team that does the work should be as small as possible. Small is beautiful, and effective. Don't start inviting everyone to the organisation. Only people who have an *added value* and will spend a *significant* amount of time to the project can be in the core organisation. Try to avoid going overboard on working groups. Working groups can drown a project in communication overhead. If there should be that much discussion anyway, postpone the project and first make up the minds.

Next to the people who do the work, are the people that have some influence on it, but do nothing; a large part of the stakeholders. The project organisation can be used to satisfy some wishes of stakeholders to create the much needed win-win situations. In its most simple form, you can create a project trashcan ("The Project Tactical Non-Binding Advisory Committee") where you put in the people who just want to be involved in the project (to save their territory), but which you have no use for.

Be creative while constructing the project organisation. Take the Bob Ross way to paint your organisation: "This is a sweet little project staff. I put it here next to the tracking and control group, so it has a friend."

## 2.12. Be a winner yourself

And now you have read all this paperwork. You talked with all those people. You asked "what do you want?". "What can I do?" Now it's time for your gut feeling.

Do you trust the statements made by the stakeholders? Do you think top management will stick with you? Do you honestly believe the project has a chance to succeed?

Now is the time to know. It is late, but you can still get off the train. After this, it's your ass that's on the line. When this project is mentioned, it's your face the people see.

It makes no sense to associate yourself with a project if you think it's a Titanic or Mission Impossible IV. Don't make the mistake thinking your effort will be appreciated, even if everything goes down the drain. Failure is an easy thing to remember. The true professional knows his limitations, and the only responsible thing to do is, either configure the project in such a way it stands a chance, or return it to the sender.

A quote is always great, but this one from US judge Jackson to Microsoft during the trial over their monopoly position is in this context even perfect:

*"The code of tribal wisdom says that when you discover you are riding a dead horse, the best strategy is to dismount. (But lawyers) often try other strategies with dead horses, including the following: buying a stronger whip; changing riders; saying things like 'This is the way we've always ridden this horse'; appointing a committee to study the horse; ...declaring the horse is better, faster and cheaper dead; and, finally, harnessing several dead horses together for increased speed."*

If you take it on, don't forget to include your own stakes: be a winner yourself!

And, if you are a winner, and higher management is committed to you as a project manager for the project, make sure they send a memo or an e-mail to all stakeholders, announcing you as the new king, the main man, the ruler of your universe…or something more "office like".

# *Chapter 3*

## *Requirements Determination*

## 3.1. Stakeholders in the mist

I have this friend who has a friend, who had a discussion with his girlfriend the other day. She accused him of not being romantic enough and that he never organised something nice for the both of them. So he replied a spineless "OK" and took her to this VERY expensive restaurant, with smooth music, wine and sophistication. She refused to go in, "cause it was too expensive and they could not afford it". He was like going "WHAT?!!"

Stop and think for a moment all the times that you thought you understood what someone was saying, and you later found out you were utterly wrong. Wilson, the neighbour of Tim Allen in Home Improvement would say: "The limitation concerns human bias in the selection and use of data. These biases arise because humans use less than optimal heuristics when retrieving and processing information." Basically, we are too narrow minded and not open enough.

At this point in a project we have to determine what the requirements are for the end result. We have to get it out of the heads of the stakeholders and on a piece of paper. For this, a lot of communication is needed between very different people. As a kid I played this little game at school we called 'telephone line'. Twenty kids were hurdled up into a circle. One started by whispering a sentence in the ear of his neighbour, so the other kids couldn't hear what was said. The neighbour would say the same sentence to his neighbour, and so on, until the sentence was 'round circle'. The fun of the game was comparing what the last one had heard with what was originally said. Mostly, they didn't even come close. Kids and stakeholders are almost the same. The sentence of the first stakeholders is often different from the software the last user will see.

The most widely used and efficient way of getting the requirements is by asking. By talking to key stakeholders, like future users of the system, the needed information will emerge. It might seem obvious that this should be as accurate as possible, however it is crucial to do it correctly at this stage. Although information systems are expensive to develop, changes made once a system has been completed are 50 to 100 times more expensive than making the same changes during the requirements determination activities.

And that's a hell of a job. We already mentioned the difficulties in understanding each other. But there is another catch also, you have to anticipate the ways the tasks will change when they are running under the new system. Watts Humphrey [1989] would even go this far in stating that…

*"requirements by their very nature cannot be firm because we cannot anticipate the ways the tasks will change when they are automated. …Unless the job has previously been done and only modest changes are needed, it is best to assume that the requirements are wrong."*

In this section the determination will be done by means of a workshop with the key stakeholders. A workshop is a kind of a discussion between key holders, with a conductor who manages the process. It is dynamic. It should be fun. Whiteboards are used. Big screens and flashy presentations. People should walk around. And, of course, this show should produce a real end product; a set of requirements.

It can be one workshop or multiple, depending of the scope of the project. This chapter will handle preparing and conducting a workshop, and what to do with its results.

One thing should be stated at this point: the workshop mentioned in this chapter aims to handle requirements made to the end result of the project (the product). Requirements made to the way the project is conducted (the process) can be handled by the same concept as described in the section.

The activities in this section are not necessarily pure project management tasks. Of course the planning part is, but conducting the workshops isn't. However, because of its importance and the impact of requirements on the complete process of the project (remember, they're still a reflection of the stakes of the stakeholders), the software project manager should at least be aware of it's pitfalls. If the project is large (read "small") enough, it is recommended that the project manager also conducts the workshop, or is present in its discussions.

## 3.2. Preparing the workshop–educating

The end result of the requirements determination activities should of course be a set of requirements. The representation of this set will be treated later on in this chapter. A point to address at this moment is the depth of it all. How far should one go into detail? There is, as you might have expected, no concrete answer. The criteria one should handle at all time is that a requirement is unambiguous, that all stakeholders have the identical view on what the requirement means. You must use your own judgement on this one. To be able to judge, you must know the tasks that will be changed as part of the project.

And that's where it all starts. *Educating the project manager*. The project manager should follow the stakeholders for a while in their daily tasks. This is the only way to get a feeling for the subjects. How urgent everything might be, take the time to do this. It will pay off in the end. It helps building a sense for the processes, for the business case, for the entire organisational context. It is important to go at the issues from these angles, the wider and broader perspective.

Most users, and other stakeholders, tend to formulate their requirements based upon their current situation. They see where they are now, and can talk about the two or three steps they want to make from their current point. This is a handicap, because it limits the possibilities. Seen from a market, business and process perspective, more opportunities could be taken. Instead of talking about "extra data fields in our customer entry screen" one should address the things one wants to do with a customer, and reason from this back to what information is needed to do it.

It sounds obvious. It is. For an information analyst this might be peanuts. But for most people it tends to be very difficult. During the actual requirements determination you need the stakeholders to be completely holistic ("Ahum, let your mind flow freely in the space that surrounds you."). So, you have to *educate the stakeholders* before starting the phase. Let them visit a seminar on the future of the market, let them brainstorm about how their job is an integral part of the company's process, whatever. Let them view their tasks as part of the whole.

## 3.3. Use the checklist

In the preparation of the workshop you can follow this checklist of aspects to consider:

- General information (title, place and time)
- Purpose
- Scope
- Subjects
- Controversy
- Strategy
- Result
- Participants
- Roles
- Tools
- Feedback/follow-up
- Agenda

In the remainder of this section the aspects will be treated in more detail. With these points you cover the basics for a successful workshop.

### General information

Starting off with some general information, your workshop's got to have a title, a name to call the beast by. Make it short, clear and not a novel…"workshop on order entry" is a good one. Pick a date and place. I will not say a thing about the place. Actually a nice book that even includes maps on how your room should look like is "Rapid Application

Development" by James Martin [1991], it's a classic, so just read the original. Concerning "time", I just want to mention that the unit of duration for a workshop should be a part of the day (two parts make one day, so morning and afternoon). Don't drag people out for one hour. That's not a workshop, that's a conversation.

## Purpose

What is the workshop all about? Purpose, scope and subjects, that's what defines the actual workshop. The purpose is important to inform the workshop participants correctly up front, so that they have no wrong expectations, or at least make the chance on that a little smaller. By the way: you don't have to yank all info into one sentence. It's ok to make a paragraph out of it. "Partial requirements in the preliminary decision making phase" is a sentence, but it tells nothing. If the requirements coming out of the workshop are not final, but will be reviewed and approved by some hot shots afterwards, write it like that! It won't give you the Nobel prize for literature, but it sure will save your workshop.

## Scope

The purpose will place the workshop within the context of the project, the scope tells us all about the actual content, e.g. "order entry for 24 hour delivery". The scope should determine the field that will be covered, including a good definition of it's borders. "How a new information system will have to support our order entry activities for 24 hour deliveries. Current activities may be subject to change." The second ("…may be subject to…") sentence is very important. If things may be altered, make them explicit, try to avoid that people have to read between the lines, or have to be sensitive to the words chosen. The opposite holds also, of course. If it's not allowed, state it. "How a new information system will have to support our order entry activities for 24 hour deliveries. The new order entry activities as described in Large Document X and approved by Big Guy Y have to be considered."

## Subjects

To create a good list of subjects to cover, some homework has to be done. A good preparation would be joining stakeholders in their work for a short time, mentioned earlier in this section. In addition to this, you should talk with someone with knowledge about the scope. A good starting point, if possible, is to take the tasks that fall into the scope. Like, for order entry…

- Getting the order
- Finding the customer
- Checking for stock
- Placing the order
- Tracking the delivery

Another way is to make a distinction in categories of the subject at hand. If you order an ad in a newspaper, you have the little public announcements and the larger display ads. You can discuss about large customers and small customers. Blue balls and yellow balls. Take your pick.

So, there are a thousand ways to organise your subjects. They should be clear, logical, "feel good" and make immediate sense to the participants.

## Controversies

"How a new information system will have to support our order entry activities for 24 hour deliveries. The new order entry activities as described in Large Document X and approved by Big Guy Y have to be considered." A purpose like that for your workshop, and you know you will have some trouble. Probably someone in the workshop is no fan of Big Guy Y. Thinks he doesn't know a thing about order taking. However, the Large Document X is approved and is the basis for the workshop. T, R, O, U, B, L, E.

Perhaps one of the workshops subjects is reorganised for the 100th time. Maybe "ISO Certification" is the "soup du jour" (hype of the day) at the company, so everyone just wants to write large documents. Possibly the same workshop has taken place last year, and no one heard a thing about that one.... Controversies on the subjects of the workshops. Find them. You really need help with this one. Again talk to people and listen to them.

## Strategy

Given the controversies and the list of subjects you put on the form in the previous steps, you should determine how to handle things, how to approach the subjects strategically. I know, I said the goal is to make everyone a winner. Take care of all stakes. But probably not every one in the workshop is feeling lucky due to the controversies. If people don't want to be concerned with the project in the first place, they can frustrate the process of conducting the workshop. If they are out to sabotage and are not into the win-win mood, you will not get them. Not during the workshop. You can handle them later on. Be pragmatic, you also need an end result, so don't let them block your workshop.

For the Big Guy Y hater, bring it as a given. This is it, you can't do a thing about it, so stop whining. Be passive, confronting, whatever flavour you have up your sleeve (smell that shirt!).

For this ISO thing, you might try making the issue bigger, bolder, more abstract. Like, if someone yaps about "documenting every thing", make it in little steps bigger: "Yeah, you are right. You should document it, and have a great structure to support that. You want every thing stored in one place. So you can access it from everywhere. But of course, to be effective, you should also register this, and that. So you can cross reference it with...." If you can avoid the sarcasm and sound sincere, they will bring up that they're not ready for it. I love this one.

The purpose of this step in the preparation of the workshop is that you think up front the strategies you might have to use. In this way, you can prepare some information or invite some one to the workshop to neutralise the controversy.

### Result

What will be there when the workshop is over? The requirements of the end result can be written down as a story, as a formal specification in some cryptic scientific notation, or some cool graphics. There is so much research done on this subject. How to check the set of inconsistencies? How to create a graph from Here To Eternity?

Just use the medium the key stakeholders are used to. If they like to tell stories, tell a story. If they are mathematicians, use formal calculus. If they are computer scientists, use bloody graphs. I like to tell stories myself.

Specify how the result will look like. How you can read it. Close your eyes, and see it!

### And finally, the rest

To close your preparation, you can specify the participants of the workshop. Who are they, what is their position within the organisation, and, most important, why are they invited for the workshop; what role do they play in the discussions; leader, chairman, scribe…

If you want to use tools, you should write them down, and arrange that they are there.

This one deserves some emphasis: *On which way will the results be communicated back to the participants, and what are the next steps for these results?*

And only at this stage, you are able to create an agenda for the workshop. Only here, at the end of the preparation you have enough information to create a good agenda.

Enough swimming on the side of the lake, let's jump in.

## 3.4. Conducting the workshop

You are standing in front of a room. You are not alone. There are more people in the room. Some you know, some you don't. They all stare at you. You have an idea what they are thinking. Or at least you think you do as you prepared this workshop as described. These people come here to defend their ground, to conquer new ones, to enhance power, to reduce influences from others, or just basically to kill time.

Thinking back about the Flow of stakes, you remember what you are supposed to do. You have to fulfil everyone's wishes today. The people in the room have their issues, their stakes, and they will project it on the topic of the day.

If you are trying to defend your department's independence, you will not be happy with an information system that integrates all processes and makes your employees, or at least the things they do, obsolete. You want to have separate systems for all processes, and your empire in between. You will probably use a different argument. Terms like 'easier to maintain', 'better to control', and 'more transparent' will more likely be used.

## Formulate requirements

So there you are, sweating in front of the room. You have to formulate, together with the members of the workshop, the requirements for the end result of the project. It's a software project; a system will be a large part of this end result. This set of requirements should address all the stakes of the stakeholders, and, in the same time, not be conflicting to each other. If one requirement says the button should be blue, and another it should be green, you will have requirements that you know will be impossible to fulfil.

This sounds difficult. It actually is. But, with enough time and patience, you can get a long way. But time is normally not on your side, and you should actually try to get a reasonable set at the end of the workshop. Compromises, concessions and a little force enter the mix of actions of the project manager. Everybody should be a winner, and today!

Can you satisfy all the needs of every one? Can you take care of all their stakes? Can you make every one happy on this day? Probably not everyone. If people don't want to be concerned with the project in the first place, they can frustrate the process of conducting the workshop. If they are out to sabotage and are not into the win-win mood, you will not get them. Today. You can handle them later on. You cannot tolerate them having an impact on the flow of the workshop. They should not have been invited anyway. Sometimes, sadly, you have to. But you can block it by having some colleague sitting in that also feels differently about the subject. Or a senior manager, who shuts him or her up.

## Focus on allies

Two important pieces of advise come from D'Herbemont and Cesar [1998]. First: focus on your allies. If you have to get some points across, and people are against it, the natural reaction is to win them over by paying a lot of energy to them. Instead, you should support the people who agree on the matter in convincing the disbelievers. In this way you have more people to spread the word and mostly from the same environment as the 'don't wanna's'. And we all have the tendency to accept something faster from someone out of the same environment, then from a total stranger.

The second tip is to create lateral projects. Try to formulate the project or end result in such a way that it appeals to a specific group of people. Perhaps you have to focus differently or to include some stuff to make it interesting. It's a good and funny mechanism to work with.

## Getting the right information

How can you get the right information out of the people that are in front of you (remember, you are hosting a workshop)? I thought about this complex question for a long time. I came up with one answer: ask.

If you know from yourself that you are no talker, introvert and have problems with your communication skills, this workshop leader thing is nothing for you. If you have them, be yourself and just ask.

Here are some strategies that work for me.

- *Be stupid.* Don't be a smart ass. Even if you already know all of it, let the participants be the stars. They are the experts.
- *Ask what you know.* Start for example with asking something you already know. Tell something you know is not correct. Try to get the attention and see who corrects what. Most of the time it gives you some glimpse of stakes.
- *Repeat.* If some one tells you what, just repeat what he said, but using different words. In this way, you can get similarity in words used.
- *Ask 5 times.* Ask five times why. That will give you the highest level of reason. Ask 5 times how, and it will bring you to the lowest level of operation.

While the workshop leader is going through the process from left to right and top to bottom, the scribe should record all the statements made. Every statement should have a label who said it. In distribution of the statements, and, later on, the requirements, the name should always appear. This will keep people committed to what they said. If they just yell something, and their name is attached to it, the will be more careful what to say.

At the end of each day, for example, at least at the end of the workshop, the statements should be reviewed by the participants and be approved. Group statements together by subject, try to rephrase them with the participants so that they use the same 'language' and try to avoid, or at least clarify, conflicting statements. The last action is to mark statements as requirement, and try to establish some priorities in them. A mechanism often used is to classify requirements as 'must-have', 'nice-to-have' and 'oh-well-this-is-just-a-suggestion'.

I stated in the beginning of this section, the purpose of the workshop is to establish requirements on the end result of the project (the product, which may also include organisational issues and procedures). However, some times statements are made on the way the project will be conducted (the process). Create a separate list for these statements, and provide them to project management for consideration. But make sure you tell the workshop participants that these process-statements are treated differently.

## 3.5. Representing the requirements

You have all your requirements in front of you on a piece of paper. You smell the paper. You feel the paper. You sense the emotions that are attached to the requirements. You close your eyes, and you have these images, these colourful blurs, you are in touch with the minds of the stakeholders. You are the stakeholder profiler. You have to get the stakes out of the requirements.

Group all the requirements together per stakeholder. Try to formulate the stakes that are behind them. It's difficult, it's rather vague, it's very "soft", but it's the information you are after. Remember, the requirements will likely change during the course of the project, but stakes remain the same.

The requirements itself will be represented in the way you defined in the preparation of the workshop. All the participants will have their own version, and are confronted with the stuff they wished for; every requirement has a name attached to it who said it.

For project management and perhaps some key stakeholders, it may be wise to have some representation of the stakes. Such a presentation may help to refine the definition of the stakes. Taken from a professional FBI profiler, you could use some great slides with, for every stakeholder, a photo and the crimes (stakes) he or she committed.

**Stakeholder profile**

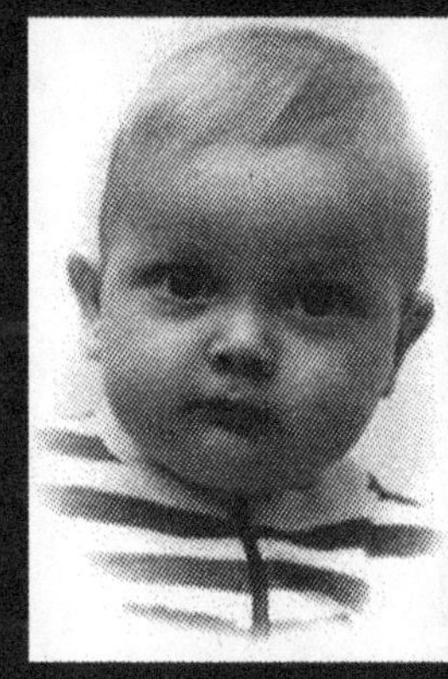

Name: *Bas de Baar*

Position: *author*

Stakes: *Wants to be... a) a millionaire, b) liked*

Sponsor: *Simone*

# Chapter 4

## Requirements Validation

## 4.1. Feedback time!

How many times did you order in a restaurant this very nice meal, which was described on the menu as delicious, to later find out the cook went completely experimental on it? I read this incredibly great description for a main course involving the better parts of a lamb. When I got it, I noticed it wasn't actually cooked; I like my meat extremely well done, nuked to the bone. I remembered, a menu is not a meal.

How many times did you bring your car to the garage for a check up, to hear later on from the mechanic that he took special care of the noise he heard? You are going deaf, or this guy is hearing sounds that are not there, anyway you have to pay for this extra 'service'.

How many times are kids getting a dog because "I wanna doggie" is yelled by some 10 year old, so that the kid can later realise he didn't want the doggie itself, but the soft feeling of fur? You may think you want it, to find out later you had no idea what you were actually wishing for. Having the kid itself falls into this category.

How many times must a man…

### Meanwhile, back in the jungle…

In the jungle of software project management the fierce full application developer is searching for requirements. After a good hunt he is dragging a bag full of statements back to his cave. There he grunts for weeks, he picks every requirement up, looks at it, smells it and takes it apart. After months, the creature sets foot for the first time outside his cave. The daylight is hitting hard on him. With him he drags a large ball made out of pieces of requirements. The pastry is the results of his craftsmanship. He shows it to the rest of the tribe. Holding it up, shining in the sun. The tribe leader looks at it, smells at it, sets fire to it. Anthropologists are still trying to figure out, if the leader communicated his disapproval or that he provided warmth to the tribe.

## Expectations

The central issue here is "expectations". You imagine a certain situation in the nearby future. You close your eyes and you can actually experience it. You open them again, and try to describe what you saw to some one else. He will hear the same words, the same sentences and you might even share the same enthusiasm for it. But if you both think about "a nice woman" or "a nice man", you both having the same warm feeling doesn't guarantee you that the colour of the hair of the imaginary friend is identical. It probably isn't. Communication is always influenced by interpretation of a person. Requirements in a software project are not different in this respect. An "easy to use interface" can be interpreted in hundreds of ways.

So, there is nothing you can do? Wrong. You can do a lot, but it will take some effort. You can provide feedback by using a mechanism, which is not affected by interpretation, or at least less affected. Exchanging pictures of your idea about "a nice (wo)man" can solve the hair colour issue. There are several available you can use on the product requirements of a software project. And that's what this section is all about.

## Good idea, bad idea

It's not only the talking with people that can cause problems. It's also your own imagination that plays tricks on you. What may seem nice in your head, me be in reality a disaster. Even if the other person understood you correctly. Feedback is also here the magic word. It can help indicate that you, or any one else, was wrong with his idea of the future at a relatively early time in the project.

Requirements validation is all about feedback. Is the interpretation of the requirements to the real life situation correct, and, are the requirements still valid? It's now "feedback time"!

## 4.2. Global to detail

In my home town the city built a complete new neighbourhood, houses, roads and parking spaces, everything is new. Even the people. I don't know how it is in the rest of the world, but in Holland, such a new area has to have a new work of art. But for $300.000 the locals should have influence on the choice of what kind of concrete with holes and circles they want to have (yep, it's called 'participation').

The first requirement is put up by city hall: the art piece should reflect the struggle between man and the water (we live at the coast you know, 'the struggle between man and the government' would be more appropriate). Next, ten artists are asked to put in their suggestions. Vague drawings of holes and squares, circles and sockets, black and blue blurbs. Intended is that the inhabitants get an idea of what they can have in front of their doors. Everybody can vote (I make no funny remarks about the US 2000 elections, and that's difficult).

The three winners go to the next round. They make a detailed work drawing of the actual construction of their art piece. Is it steel? Is it placed in water? Is it green? Is it ugly? Based upon the final drawings the government chooses. Steel, water, green, ugly? Yep, yep, yep and yep again.

### Software design

You know, creating a piece of software is also a work of art. Luckily there is no voting with the residents, otherwise no system would ever be build. But the mechanism of taking a requirement and creating first a global drawing and afterwards a more detailed sketch is similar. We wouldn't be fair to the profession if we hadn't a great name for it: a *design*.

If we have good requirements, they will not say too much on how a system should be built. It should provide us statements on what it should do, in what context, and perhaps, sometimes, how it should be performed. All technicians that read the previous chapter would have wondered "where is my design?" Well, here you are.

Designs are in fact a way of communicating how a software system should be constructed. They are a description of what will be the end result. In this way, it's one of the earliest points in time, when stakeholders can see some glimpses on what is done with their requirements. So, when all the techies go to work, the project manager should make sure they maintain relations between the design choices and the original requirements.

### Global and detail

What is global and how deep is detail? There you got me. Draw a line somewhere where you feel natural. If you look at a system as boxes, the global design places the boxes within a certain context, and their dependencies. The detailed design fills the boxes.

Another way of looking at it, is by functional versus technical aspects. The first design (or specification, for now the differences are too tiny to discuss) masters the points on how to handle the system from a user perspective; what should the user do and what will the system do? The second phase covers the technical implementation of the functional one. What data to manipulate? Which file to copy where? This approach reflects the opinion that techies can never lead the design process, the functional aspects rule!

Any way, you start your translation of the requirements to the real world by making designs or specifications. It is of course a communication tool for the technicians within their own species. But stakeholders want to see what happened with the things they yelled, and this is their first opportunity, so you better take care.

## 4.3. Designs and normal people

After reading the previous section, I know you get my point. However, I will spend some more text on the matter, because it's too important, and the natural tendency within software projects is to consider designs as a product of their own. "We design to create a design." Wrong, wrong, wrong. A design is a medium to tell how the requirements will be translated to the real world. And there lies the problem for project management with specifications and designs; the designs are considered to be a word passed from one technician to another. The global expert, tells the detailed expert, who tells the developer what to do. And they pass their message by the medium 'design'. They leave out the non-technicians, the 'normal' people…

During the actual construction of the specifications the software project manager will not be involved too much in the discussions. And if he is, it's not because he has the role of project manager. The biggest challenge for the manager is to make sure the communication to the stakeholders is done effectively and timely. He should make sure that once in a while the software gurus come out of their cave and tell in understandable words what they are envisioning. These discussions are legendary, two different worlds meet each other. Try to order something in Paris and you catch the drift.

## Enhancing the chance of success

The project manager can do something to enhance the chance of success of this process. First, to be aware…and that you are now. Second, the choice of the guy or gal leading the design activities should not be solemnly based upon his technical know-how, communicative skills weigh even stronger. And, last in the 'open-door' series, take more time for the specifications than you think you need. Take the time to create designs. You will earn it back later on. However, use the extra time for communicating with the stakeholders, not to make your graphics look more slick.

The communication between the designers and the stakeholders can take place in workshops and other kinds of meetings. So, the project manager, that means you, can check if such meetings are planned and held, or can even actively schedule such sessions or emphasise the need for them. After such a meeting is held, schedule a talk with one of the stakeholders to see if he got the information he wanted.

## Document it all

To ensure that the information is presented in such a way, that the stakeholders can understand the specifications, the designers should keep track of all the decisions they made, and, more importantly, the arguments why they made a certain decision. If they decide to use Super XMLParser sub-system GNA (don't try to find this one) somewhere should be recorded that they intend to use it, and further more, the arguments on why this sub-system and not an other one. If they talk with normal people, then at least they can keep up the appearance of knowing what they are doing, to be aware of their actions.

But stakeholders just want to know one thing: "What the heck happened to my requirements?" So, the next log the designers have to keep is the one containing relations between the design decisions and the requirements issued. A paragraph in a design on the generation of an error log file in HTML on some server, should be linked to have an "easy to access medium to verify incorrect responses of export to the other system." The latter being an example of a requirement. In preparation for one of the feedback meetings a designer just has to see who's coming, extract their requirements and present the information on what he did with them. That's feedback especially tailored to suit you.

As a closing remark for this section, remember that designing is an iterative process; you design, you discuss, you throw stuff away and put new consideration into it. You win some, you lose some. Keep this in mind, when you design the process to perform these activities. Brooks [1995] even states that you have to plan to throw one away. You will in the end anyway!

## 4.4. Get it signed

Once in a while we have these live debates of our government on television (remember I'm Dutch). It's a rare chance to see democracy in action. Party A states something. Party B is "in principle not negative in respect to the suggestion". Party C "can imagine an agreement with consideration of aspects that are currently not known, but could arise in the future, possibly, or not all." You watch this soap opera and you think they all agree. You thought wrong. Weeks later, they have the same discussion and you have the idea that they don't agree. Wrong. They do. Do they? And after four years of discussion we get a new government.

Ever have this meeting where during the meeting you are quite sure that you know where the other guy is standing? That you exactly know what his opinion is? You walk out of the room, you drive home and you reflect on the meeting and can't remember an exact statement that supports your feeling? If you haven't, just do a software project and you will.

### Get it signed!

It's very important that the stakeholders get the feedback from the designers, but it is in the same level of importance that the project manager gets the feedback that the stakeholders were happy (or unhappy) with what they saw. Don't forget, you, the software project manager are also a stakeholder, and you should also take care of your stakes. You have to make sure you make progress within the project. That small steps are taken in the right direction, and you got to have this feedback in a non disputable way. You just have to get it signed!

After some feedback to the stakeholders, let them sign that they agree on what they saw. That what they saw, takes care of their requirements. If they state "That's a nice design", your answer has to be "That's nice, please sign here." If people are forced to make a formal commitment to a piece of paper (or electronic equivalent of paper), they read more carefully before they commit, and after signing they stick longer to their statement. It's not a matter of cost, we will handle that in the next section, but it's a way of getting some stable points in an otherwise dynamic (or chaotic) environment.

### Get it signed!

Of course, the procedure of what to sign should be in relation to the size of the project. It doesn't make sense to sign every paragraph, but don't wait until the end, when everything is ready. Get intermediate approvals.

In some weird way, most people are reluctant to put their commitment on paper. It's just a signature. But the request alone can be considered an insult. "My word should be good enough for you." Well, actually it shouldn't. Never trust a used car salesman who says "trust me". If you can't get in place a good approval structure, leave the project, go home, you loose in the end. Every one will bend and twist and everything will move consistently, with the exception of yourself. Remember, you are a stakeholder, so take care of your own stakes.

While you are in this process, just think of one thing: *GET IT SIGNED*!

## 4.5. Giving it a try

I ask myself sometimes questions like "You know the software business. You know how systems are built. Are you now comfortable, sitting in this airplane, 10km high in the sky, flying on systems that some software geezer constructed?" Uuuhhhr, honestly I don't know. The best thing is not to think about it too much.

What I know is this: after designs are made (or even during) software engineers have to try things out. They are not always sure that certain concepts can be done at all, or wonder how it will act in reality. To stay in the language used in this course: they need feedback on the parts and principles they are supposed to implement. And these trials are not always thrown away…like they should.

## Pilot, prototype and Hollywood

Brooks [1995] has a very clear opinion on this matter:

*"The management question, therefor, is not whether to build a pilot system and throw it away. You will do that. ...Delivering that throwaway to customers buys time, but only at the cost of agony for the user, distraction for the builders while they do the redesign, and a bad reputation for the product that the best redesign will find hard to live down."*

You will create pilots for trying things out, but the pilots are focussed on this particular aspect that they are attempting to prove. They are *not* designed as a part of a whole, which makes them a nightmare to use in a complete system.

But before throwing them away, these exercises are crucial for your project. They provide at an early stage the first glimpses of the requirements in a product. If you take a trip to Hollywood you should visit the Universal Studios. There you can be guided through the studios. You will see all those little streets you can see in movies and TV series. Even standing before a building, you can appreciate the look and feel, you can sense the ambience. If you turn the corner, you see that the street consists of only the front of the houses. Disappointed? No. The mock-ups serve their purpose.

A prototype is a mock-up of software, a Hollywood system. You can use it in an early stage to give users a sense of what the end will look like. Mostly it's just a window with buttons that don't do anything. But a user can mentally walk through the system. Don't forget to tell them it's a mock-up, to avoid later disappointment. Feedback time! And if they like it, get it signed!

## Proof of concept and benchmarks

A couple of years ago I did a project where we implemented a system that consisted of multiple remote databases that had to be synchronised. Perhaps for you that is peanuts, but at that time we had no experience in this concept. Ok, it was done elsewhere, so it had to be possible. The supplier of the software had done a small exercise in this area with an administrative system they used internally for tracking the projects. It consisted of one central database and small databases on laptops of the engineers. This provided a perfect feedback to the customer that the concept could be done, a so called, *proof of concept.*

However, scepticism arose on the scalability of the concept. It might perform well with a few users and data, but how does this perform with heavy data traffic and hundreds of users? This matter was handled by building a pilot(!) that just synchronised databases with a lot of data, and a simulated workload of a user making updates and queries. The time it took for results came back for the simulated user, and the time it took to synchronise (and some other technical measurements) were used as a reference for the future system. It was considered a *benchmark.* Those measurements on the pilot were acceptable, so the system to build was regularly checked against the benchmark. It provided a feedback on the scalability and on how far the actual system was away from the acceptable measurements.

### Plan it

The activities described in this section, they will be performed. It is how software people must work, and it is how you can provide proper feedback to your stakeholders. Listen to Brooks: don't deliver the throwaway as a final system, you will lose in the end. It will happen, so plan it in advance, make it an official part of your project.... Plan time to try things out, you will, anyhow!

## 4.6. Testing, one-two-three, testing

In the previous section the main focus is on having feedback on principles, ideas and look-and-feel. You need this. But it's only the start of it all. While engineers are building the system (or merely configuring it), extensive testing has to be done. Does it work, and does it work properly? You might perhaps consider this as not being part of the feedback loop to the stakeholders, but consider the requirements "it has to work" and "I don't want to reboot my system three time a day". If these requirements are explicitly stated, you are lucky, mostly people *assume* that it speaks for itself (pity the poor fools!).

## Technical testing

As a project manager you have to be aware that testing happens. Not just checking if by pressing the button the wheel spins, but also looking if the roof is not collapsing because there happens to be some relation between the wheel and the roof (yeah, a far fetched example). Look if the parts are tested, and the whole of the parts. Don't trust developers if they say they don't need testing ("*software is like bananas; they ripen at the customer*"); it's a complex task and the discipline is just a few decades old. By the way, it is a discipline, that starts at the level of the individual developer.

## Functional testing

This technical stuff is all fine, but what happens if the system (or parts of it) comes available from the developers? You now have to test of it is functional. Does it perform what is supposed to, and in a way it is supposed to? It is the big final feedback to the stakeholders.

To do this properly you have to prepare in advance. Think of the real life situation of the system in the future, and come up with some scenarios that can be considered as an archetype situation. Try to write scenarios (including human aspects and handling) that cover all the major aspects.

When testing an editorial system for newspapers (the big word processors on steroids) role-play is used to construct all archetype pages, including someone writing, someone correcting etc. This is the big acceptance test. You need therefor to construct the scenarios with all stakeholders concerned. If the system passes the test, they just have to sign for final acceptance.

## 4.7. Rolling with the punches

In this chapter I described this pandemonium where everyone is sharing, "show me yours, I'll show you mine", and in general providing feedback. I discussed the need for feedback, and some ways the feedback can be given. The result of it all is change. Changing requirements, changing realisation of these requirements. I quoted before: "*Unless the job has previously been done and only modest changes are needed, it is best to assume that the requirements are wrong.*"

There are several reasons why requirements change:

- *Stakeholder changes his mind.* By discussing, thinking about it and reflecting on the subject, a stakeholder can change his mind on what he wants.
- *Project team interpreted requirements different than intended by stakeholder.* Two people don't understand each other.
- *"Forgotten" requirements pop up.* During the project intake and the requirements determination the scope is determined and the initial requirements are written down. In this process you can forget one or two requirements that appear during the phase of feedback.
- *Changes in the project surroundings.* Things happened outside the project that can affect the project directly. A merger or reorganisation, a new policy for buying supplies, a new law, etc. The fluctuation in the surroundings can change requirements. The longer a project runs, the more vulnerable the project is to this type of changes.

The software project manager has to roll with the punches; these changes are a fact-of-project-life, so he has to deal with it. However, to be able to construct something, requirements should be relatively stable, at least long enough to build and test stuff.

This stability, can be forced by not allowing changes to the requirements, they are frozen. Requirements in a project will have alternating periods of change and freeze. It's the role of the project manager to manage this process. It's called "change control": the process by which a change is proposed, evaluated, approved or rejected, scheduled and tracked.

The key issue is to install a change control procedure that forces people to go to one central point of entry for the project. E.g. project management will decide if a change in the requirement set is accepted or rejected. Only one person is allowed to change the set of requirements. This is one procedure I really recommend putting in place.

# Chapter 5

## *Project Progress*

## 5.1. On the move

In October 2000 I went for the first time to the US. Together with my then girlfriend, I flew to Las Vegas for a month's trip into Nevada and California. We married in Las Vegas and afterwards hit the road towards Reno, NV.

I had spoken to a lot of people before we took the trip. They told me "you can drive there for hours and don't see anyone". Being from Western Europe I thought "yeah, sure, right". In my area the best you can do is not seeing anyone for 10 minutes in the neighbourhood of nuclear waste disposals. So, I hit the road Jack. Rental car, newly wed wife next to me, climate control to the max, Rick James funkin' from the CD-player, driving through Nevada. You know these postcards where you just see a road going straight to the horizon and then disappear, with nothing but nature next to it? That's what I got for two days.

When they mean nothing, they really mean *nothing*. I had most of the time no idea how far I was, how much time I needed for getting gas, coming to a town bigger then two houses. Just this one road, and once in a very long while you hit upon a landmark (e.g. old mine), and I was able to determine "ok honey, we can go to a bathroom within 2 or 4 hours." The advantage of one road is, you cannot go wrong. No exits, no decisions, no errors.

Driving from Las Vegas to Reno is easy compared to driving from my hometown to a customer I once worked for. It's only 50km distance, but full of turns and twists, detours and uncharted roads on newly built industrial areas. Every 500 meters you have to make a decision.

### Driving Miss Project

Project progress is all about driving the project on the road towards its final destination. Where are we and how long do we still have to go? Attached to the answers of these questions are the requirements of the stakeholders towards the process of the project: Are we still within budget? Do we make it on time?

The *project progress* is an indicator relative to the path from the start to the estimated end, is an indicator where you are on this path, it's always a comparison between two situations, e.g. the start and the end. *Project status* on the other hand, is a description of a certain moment in time, it's a snapshot of a particular situation. Status is "we spend $300,-", progress is "we spend now 40% of our total budget, and we are on 30% of the total duration".

### Feedback all over again

I hope you first read the previous chapter on requirements validation. There the issue was giving feedback on the product requirements. In this section the mantra is "giving feedback on process requirements". And frankly, the experience is that this particular feedback loop is the more appreciated one, it's high profile, if you really succeed in this one, your career is set. So, it's a good way of helping your own stakes.

In this chapter I will talk about schedules and budgets, just simply because it's the way to communicate the feedback on the project progress. I will even go this far in yapping on Gantt, not because "Gantt *is* project management", but just for the fact that it's an accepted way of communicating; most of the time it's even because some stakeholders *do* believe "Gantt *is* project management", and it's always easier to communicate within the expectation of the other party.

But remember, it's feedback time all over again.

## 5.2. Preparing feedback-schedule

If you check your bank account, it's not because you want to see just the numbers; I assume that you are not a kind of number fetishist that gets his or her kicks from watching numbers on a piece of paper (if you are.... then these are especially for you: 633677290.... oooh, aaaah). With the state of your finance you can determine how much you still can buy, how much you can give away to charity, etc. It provides you info over how much you can satisfy your own stakes.

The project progress provides information for the stakeholders that issued requirements to the process, to the way the project is conducted. Although I encountered some financial people that come very close to fetishism, keep in mind during this entire section that it's not the numbers that are important, but the impact of the numbers on the stakes.

## Road to nowhere

To determine the progress, in time and in money, you got to have some roadmap. For time this is a *schedule* and for money this is a *budget.*

The schedule itself is not that difficult; it's a list of tasks, start and end date, who will perform the task, what will be the effort. Getting the schedule is something else, but, as everything in this course, no rocket science. A good starting point for creating the schedule is the project strategy you created during the intake. You have some phases and you need now to fill in these phases with some details. And that's where the WBS comes in.

WBS does not stand for "What a BS", well...sometimes it does, but normally it's a "*work breakdown structure*". You take a piece of paper and you set on top of it the tasks you must perform. Under it you write the tasks that make up this higher task, it's actually a more detailed description of the first task. And you can do this for every other task, resulting in a nice tree shape structure of tasks.

How far in detail should you go? There is no definitive answer to this question. Enough detailed to provide you with insight in the tasks that have to be performed, but not to the level of tasks that will take 2 hours to perform. That kind of detail is too much, it can even get the flexibility out of your approach, if during the project you find out you forgot something, or things are not going as you anticipated. This is a mistake encouraged by some stakeholders who are happy to see a WBS of 15 pages, thinking that the project manager has anticipated everything.

I read somewhere this comment of a project manager:

"My personal rule of thumb is this: If I can't fit the key tasks and milestones on a regular size sheet of paper and still read it, it's time to delegate part of the planning."

## Milestones or Millstones?

With the phases and the WBS you can construct a list of tasks to be performed. Picking the dates for the tasks is an estimation problem, which we will handle later on. But how do you handle a list of tasks? How do you control the schedule? The answer is to have *milestones*.

Milestones are events with a specific date in the schedule, that function like a kind of beacon. They represent a state of the project that is unambiguous. You are there, or you are not there. You know those computer games where you have to race and pass all these checkpoints within a certain time frame? In a project we call them milestones.

Actually, all there is to say about milestones is in the following quote from Brooks [1995 ]:

*"For picking the milestones there is only one relevant rule. Milestones must be concrete, specific, measurable events, defined with knife-edge sharpness. Coding, for a counterexample, is "90 percent finished" for half of the total coding time. Debugging is "99 percent complete" most of the time. "Planning complete" is an event one can proclaim almost at will.*

*Concrete milestones on the other hand, are 100-percent events. "Specifications signed by architects and implementers," "source coding 100 percent complete, keypunched, entered into disk library", "debugged version passes all test cases". These concrete milestones demark the vague phases of planning, coding, debugging."*

## 5.3. Preparing feedback-budget

The Europeans discovered America by accident. When they sailed over the ocean, they sudden stumbled upon some land. The first times they encountered the native inhabitants they used rum to keep from being scalped. On their next journey they came prepared; they brought beans and mirrors to trade with the Indians.

So, the Europeans gave generously the mirrors and other colourful shiny stuff in exchange for the land. However, there was so much land and so much tribes to encounter, they had no idea how much to take with them. After some experience, the Spanish, Portuguese and the Dutch could give a good estimate how much to bring with them to take all the land. They evolved even some kind of metric: five beans for 5 square miles of land. The confiscation of land took a pace never seen before. Later on, they discovered that they could not take all the beans and mirrors they needed, so they took guns instead.

The less important lesson history is trying to teach us here, is that if you come prepared you are more efficient.

## Show me the money…

To be able to give some statement on the financial state of a project, you first have to got a clue about the expected total amount you will spend, and to know where your costs are: which parts of your project require money?

To create such an overview, or to check an already existing one, you should take the WBS you constructed for the project. For every task (or group of tasks) you determine who will do it, and what is needed (in material) to do the job. E.g. "Programming the interface" will be done by Dick and he will need a PC, programming environment and a room to work in. For each person and material you need the units (man day, square feet, etc.) and the cost per unit. For the previous example you can get the following table:

| Item | Amount | Unit | Cost/unit | Total |
|---|---|---|---|---|
| Dick | 5 | day | $1000 | $5000 |
| PC | 1 | piece | $2000 | $2000 |
| Programming environment | 1 | piece | $899 | $899 |
| A room | 20 | sq.feet | $10 | $200 |

For your budget you have to cluster the costs that are similar in type. So hardware, software, infrastructure, personnel project costs (you know, the cost of Dick and the like) and training for example. This is to avoid having 20 pages of costs to get an overview of the budget, it's a kind of summary.

## 5.4. Saving to put your system through college

*"Son, what do you want to do when you grow up?"*

*"Well, dad, I have no idea. Because I'm just 8 years old I haven't evaluated my options yet. Hormonal changes will probably alter my preferences and with the pace of development in technology, it's hard to say what kind of new jobs will emerge in the future anyway."*

If your kid creates a sentence like this, be afraid, be very afraid…

A 'normal' child would just say: "Fireman, dad." Dad will smile, open a trust fund to put his son through college in the future, and will not slap him when on the kids' 20th birthday finishes his first year in medical school. That's a familiar situation!

Now Dad talks to his boss…

*"Well, Project Manager (a.k.a. Dad), when will it be ready, and what will it cost?"*

*"Boss, I have no idea. The 'it' you are referring to is undefined, the requirements are changing. The responsibilities are unclear, new people are assigned to the project from the user groups every day. It's best I take it one day at a time, we go incremental. I can tell you what the first increment will cost and when it will be ready…but don't ask me how many increments it will take. If we ever finish at all."*

Should be familiar also. Dad is a professional Software Project Manager, he knows Planning (capital intended) and has learned by experience that if he can't keep the promise, he will not provide one. Funny though, that the two 'familiar' scenario's involve the same man.

Why it is funny? Even though he knows that the changes his son becoming an actual fireman will be slim, Dad is satisfied with the answer and saves money based upon whatever assumptions he has. He has no idea if his son will go to college, if so, when, and he has no clue what it will actually cost at that time. But still, he reserves money for the future of his son.

What might be Dads problem with 'it', which happens to be an information system? The answer provided to his boss is honest and probably the truth. However, his boss is not waiting for such an answer, he must have some statements to be able to run his business. So, even though his statements are true (let's assume), is it fair to claim that you have no idea?

Fair to whom? To himself…well, he made his point; he told the exact view he has in his mind. But is it fair to just consider his own well being? Should he provide some statements to his Boss although he is highly unsure? Actually, the overall well being of the company is also in Dad his interest; if it goes bankrupt, he has no job (and his son will have no college fund). To keep the business healthy, the Boss has to have some vision on the future…. How long will my people be involved in this project (so, out of their day-to-day operations). How much money do I have to reserve for this endeavour (you know, income and expenses should be inline with each other to run a business)? So, in his own interest he should provide some statements, just like his son.

Consider why his Boss needs the claims for the future. First of all to anticipate expenses and extra resources, but also, to determine the overall course. All related activities within the company should be in tune with the strategy of this project. It's like crossing the ocean, you don't have to know the exact path you will sail, but just knowing that you aim to hit the coast at the opposite side, will help you plan a welcoming committee at the other end. Some kind of vision will help the Boss steer the *complete* business in a direction, which will benefit Dad, his project, and the stability of his job, so in the end will help raising his son.

## 5.5. Telling time

"How long would it take you to walk the marathon?" If some one asked me this question, am I able to answer it? I never walked 42 kilometres, but I think so. I once did half a marathon, so I have some indication (believe me, this was years ago). I would just multiply that time by two and add a little thing. So, although I didn't do the job previously, I can give a reasonable estimation on the duration.

"How long would it take to make your own dress?" If some one asked me this question, I am in trouble. First, I would be worried by the question itself, and second, even if I tried, I would be unable to give you a proper estimate. I would know how to make a small web site. I would know how to make a excellent spaghetti. My best guess would be something in between the site and the pasta.

Yep, we are now talking all about estimating. So, pick up the dice, and start rolling them...

### Getting an estimate

You created already a nice WBS and put some millstones (just kidding, milestones) in them. That's just fine. It is a nice structure, but it tells you nothing about the most important part of a schedule; time. Some one has to yell some dates, how long will it take, when can you start?

The best people to provide you with an estimate, are the people who will have to perform the task. First of all, they probably know what they are talking about. But most of all, it will be their estimation. Otherwise, if you have to work with the people later on in the project, and you provided the estimate, they normally will not agree and will not feel committed to do the work in your estimated time. Getting a good estimate from e.g. a programmer is not just a task for the programmer himself. The project manager plays a critical role in getting quality numbers. He has to talk with the guy (or gal), to see why he thinks it will take 7 days.... Because he already walked half a marathon, or because he thinks a dress and spaghetti are the same to create. I know, I repeat myself. I already stated this before. But, just do it, for…sake.

So, the project manager is a kind of shrink for the programmers. That's right. They just have to kick back and tell what comes to their minds, and that's it. Yeah, right, duh! The programmer, in this case, should take steps to ensure that his estimates are getting more and more accurate. He can do this by keeping statistics on how much time he spend on what. How accurate were his previous estimates, etc.

I dug this quote up on an internet newsgroup:

*"My experience is that people work to deadlines. If an engineer estimates a task will take 4 weeks, they do *not* mean 4x40=160 Hrs. They mean its feasible that it will be done 4 weeks after the start, and the Engineer will put in as many or few hours as necessary to get it done.*

*On one hand, the Engineer will be factoring in such things as other workload going on, planned days off, etc. On the other, most people will underestimate the time it actually takes, and the experienced manager will know how to "pad" (or in some cases shrink) the estimate based on the track record of the individual."*

## 5.6. Gantt and PERT

### Gantt; Icon of Project Management

If you take all you tasks from the WBS, and your estimates how long they will take and, when they could start and finish, you have the ammunition to create one of the icons of project management: The Gantt Chart. It is a good way to visualise to information you have before you. And, because it's considered an Icon, using it in your communication will set some stakeholders at ease. Basically, Gantt is an overview of tasks. You put weeks, days or months at one side, and the tasks at the other. You draw fat lines to indicate the period the task will be performed.

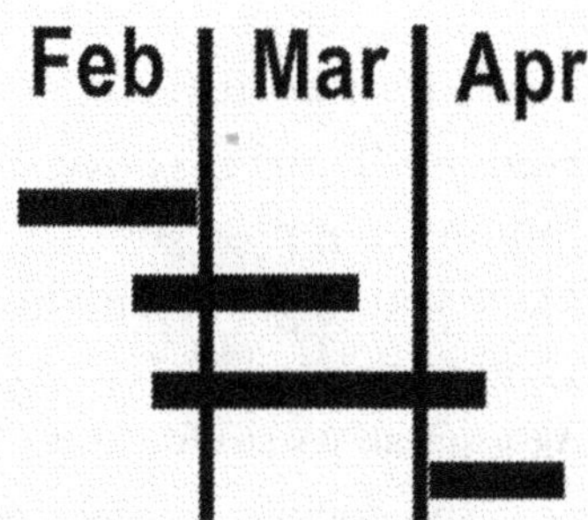


Put next to the task the name of the person who will do the job, and you come a long way.

**PERT; almost as good as Gantt**

If Sesamestreet has Bert and Ernie, Project Management has PERT and Gantt…PERT is a notation technique, which has a lot of fun features I will not discuss. The good thing however on creating a PERT chart is that you have to think about the relations between tasks. Can task X start before task Y? Do they have to end together? Must they start at the same time? etc. If you think in this way about your tasks you can create graphs like shown below.

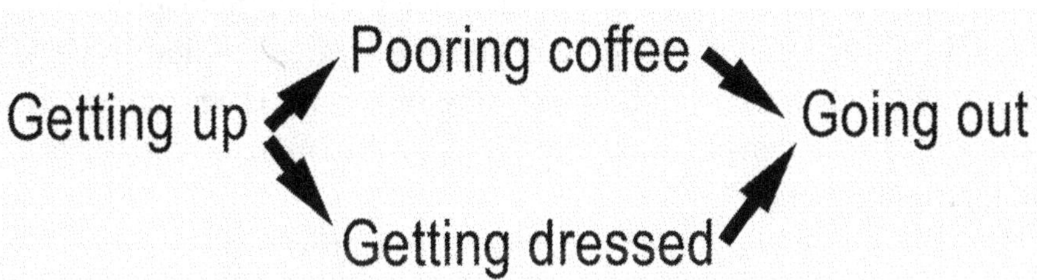


Before you can pour your coffee, you have to get up. Before you can get dressed, you have to be up. You don't have to be dressed to pour the coffee. However, you have to be dressed and had your coffee before you can leave for the office.

Suppose "Pouring coffee" takes you 5 minutes, and "Getting dressed" 15 minutes. Suppose your wife pours your coffee. In that case the time it will take you to get up and leave home is the total time for "Getting up" + "Getting dressed" + "Going out". Say, that is 30 minutes.

As long as your wife stays under the 15 minutes, you have no delay. Only if she decides to make you an espresso, you are late. You see why? This is very useful information. Not for the example I used, but for the project you have to take on. It shows you who has to wait for who, and stuff like that. It shows that a delay of one task, does not automatically mean a delay of the entire project. All the tasks that have this property however, are called the "Critical Path". These activities have to be done sequentially, will take the longest in that time frame, and a delay in one of the tasks within the critical path, will cause a delay in the entire project.

## 5.7. Tardis Wallpaper

*"This isn't a project plan, it's wallpaper for the Tardis you're going to need to meet these ^&*&%*& timescales."*

"Why is it a programmer has these success stories on how he constructed in his free time the most incredible foo-compiler within 2 days? Without bugs? Why is it that the same programmer cannot finish a simple dialog for a payroll system within the agreed period? A period he himself indicated (which by the way he largely exaggerated)? If it isn't going to happen any way, why does a project manager bother planning programmers?"

Ok, the previous paragraph is meant in a provocative manner. But being a software project manager these questions cross your mind. And off course, there's another view on the subject, that of the programmer…

"Why do I have the following discussion over and over with the project manager: 'I told you it would take 3 weeks-why did you cut it to 2 weeks, just because it met the quarter reporting deadline'. Why do I have to tell you that your $%^&^ plan bears so little relation to the Babylonian calendar that the rest of the world uses that you must be a ^%%&* Maya."

I know why I need a planning. It is a useful tool to communicate the tasks, time scales and dependencies within a project. It's a way to indicate the agreements with several parties on when what is ready. But why should programmers be bothered with a planning? What are the effects on them handing over a Gantt chart? Is it the right way to communicate any way? What does a programmer want from a planning?

So, I posted on an internet discussion forum this simple question: "Can you tell me why you (as a programmer) need a planning?" This section reflects some of the answers and, of course, strongly my personal view on the matter.

## Planning vs. schedule

I will use the term planning and schedule interchangeably in this section. Actually a planning can be a larger document with backgrounds, etceteras, plus a schedule (tasks, person, time). However, large documents are never read, and everyone just goes straight for the schedule. So, in most cases just the schedule is provided. That's why we can use the terms, for the sake of this section, for the same item.

## Agreement

When I order some furniture in Holland, the guys who will deliver the stuff at my home will send me a letter indicating which day they will come to my doorstep. The day for them starts at 8am and ends at 10pm. So, I take a day off and wait. Sit and wait.

Sit and wait is not my favourite waste of time. Especially on the job (I'm a fanatic, what can I say). For the projects I run, I will have some kind of planning, so I know when I can get my stuff to bring to the next guy. This next guy is also glad that I can tell him exactly when he gets the stuff he needs to do his thing. All in all, from my planning I can tell a lot of stories.

My storyboard in this respect might be a Gantt chart. I can send this chart to a fellow project manager, and he will immediately now what I mean. I use the chart also to put in how long and when a certain programmer performs a specific task. I do this to put our mutual agreement in writing. "How long will it take and when will it be ready?" "Well, it takes 1 week and I start on Monday." The Gantt will be used to let the programmer know I agree on what we agreed and let the rest of the world in on out little secret.

So, that's why I, a software project manager, send the programmer the planning in the first place. Why do I need a written agreement, and can't I be satisfied with just a telephone call? I wasn't even aware of the question, let alone the answer.... But someone posted on an internet discussion forum a fairly good answer...

You need a schedule for the programmer, otherwise he will never do the job you ask of him. Remember the first paragraph with the foo-compiler and the payroll system? This specific programmer would rather be writing a compiler then creating a non-challenging dull dialog for the payroll system. So, if you let him schedule his own stuff (or no planning at all), he will probably do the things he really likes first, internetting, chatting or taking the kids to the zoo.

If you would approach this pessimistically, issuing a schedule is the only way to provide the project manager with some power; non-delivery of a product is something that can be proven easily, and is therefor a perfect form of surveillance on the programmer. And this form of monitoring is needed, otherwise the programmer just slacks off.

I'm not completely happy with this form of reasoning, it's to darn pessimistic. But, if we are looking for a short statement on reality, this one is fairly close to it. I want to communicate to the programmer our agreement. This is still the case. I'm only wondering if providing a Gantt chart is such a smart move. I'm curious how I will respond if he answers me with something in UML or Bachus/Naur form.

## What is this thing called 'planning'?

The software project manager walks into the room. Very proud, handing over his new, fresh Gantt chart. It's shiny. The programmer looks at it. Holds it up, against the light.... The project manager wonders what the programmer is thinking.

"How do I read this? What is this?" The more experienced programmer goes straight to the second thought: "What happened to my numbers? I told him it would take 3 months, why did he slash it to 1?" Actually, this may not be a surprise if you think of the planning as a written agreement. The programmer first looks if it might have changed, by one party. The one who writes the document, has the power to change the text. And sadly, the 'text' of a schedule is very limited; there is no explanation on why things are what they are, why the estimate was changed. Decreasing someone's estimates of his own tasks, is a bad suggestion in the first place.

The handing over of the planning is the first form of feedback from the project manager on what he actually did with the estimates the programmer provided him earlier. If they're the same, the manager gained some credibility, if not, he's lost forever.

## Focus on the past, not the future

But, this large chart, does it provide some use for the programmer, besides just the line with his own tasks? Yes it does...it can provide insight in the quality of preparations for his task. The tasks after him are not of much interest, but the past, what happened before is key.

Having the right preparations is essential. Without them "...the result is that when I have to do some work, I loose a lot of time getting the preparations done (that have been 'forgotten' to take place), talking to people that I need the results NOW, doing things myself because the right person has other priorities, etc. And the result of this is that other people come to me wanting results NOW for work I didn't know I had to do...", as one programmer puts it.

### So what?

I hoped that I could say "we can throw the planning out of the Tardis, we don't need this thing". Sadly, we do. It's a way to communicate an agreement. However, if this way should be plotted on A1 with only a Gantt chart? I don't think so. I hate these charts anyway.

## 5.8. Telling costs

You will need to talk with financial guys, so I spend a section on higher mathematics.... Remember Dick? He was part of the budget to program some application: he was supposed to spend 5 days, with a total cost of $5000.

Suppose we schedule Dick to start on Monday and is planned to finish after five days on Friday. If you want to monitor the cost for Dicks' endeavour you just need to monitor the value of the *budget*: $5000, which is what is originally estimated. By the way, a complete budget, which is agreed upon by the customer is called a *baseline*. The budget might change due to discussions and new insight, however, the baseline can only chance after a signature of the customer. On Wednesday, Dick spend 3 days working on the stupid thing, so at that time the cost in reality are $1000 * 3 = $3000. This is the *actual cost.*

Dicks' manager could yell now: "the job is 60% completed!" However, the correct phrase should be "we have used now 60% of what we originally thought (budget)". Looking at the bits Dick produced, reveals that he has only done 25% of the application. So, actually the cost should be 25% of $5000 (total budget of Dick) = $1250. This value is called in "advanced PM lingo" the earned value.

What is the progress? Well, 25% of the total work to be done. Used 60% of the budget and estimated time. The question that has to be answered is "how much will it cost in the end?", "when is it actually finished?" Dick will say, he will work harder, he will make up in time. He probably will. But, not so much that the difference between budget and actual cost will vanish.

Enter the "*Estimate at Completion*" (EAC). This is a forecast of total project costs based upon how the project is currently doing, the project performance. It's something you have to calculate. Preferably with a computer. EAC is calculated by taking the total budget and divided by a performance factor (the cost performance index, which is Earned value / Actual cost ). This assumes that the percentage the project has overrun today is going to be the same percentage that it overruns at completion.

So, for Dick on this Wednesday, the following overview holds: actual cost $3000; total budget $5000; earned value $1250; cost performance index 0.417.

Which brings us to an EAC of: $5000 / 0.417 = $11,990.41.

Dick's in trouble.

## 5.9. Taking it like a 'man'

Now you can create nice spreadsheets with indices, draw tree structures that resemble your tasks, and what does this bring you? First of all, it brings you acceptance as a Project Manager. Project Managers are supposed to create such things. Many customers are not happy when their Project Manager doesn't show up with an Incredible Gantt Chart (preferably printed on A3, double sided).

Financial people want to see the numbers. What does it cost me in the end? They want to know as soon as possible. You can hit them now with the EAC. And, of course, the techniques are ok, they help you structure your mind, your information overload, your life.

Project progress reporting is only a nice job if you take care the expectations of the stakeholders are in line with the current situation. There is no such thing as good news or bad news. If you run over budget, that's bad news. If you stay under budget, that's for most companies also bad news; if you are a supplier and your consultants will do the job in less time then expected, you make less profit then expected, hence pissed stakeholders.

## Extra pot of gold

Again, like the entire message of this book, take care of the stakes. It's not just the numbers, it's the consequence of what they represent that causes negative reactions of stakeholders.

With budgets the guy or gal responsible always has to defend changes to a higher level. Consider a system that will be build for a certain business unit A. Parts of the system build for them, will be used later by five other business units. At the start of the project, business unit A has a budget for the complete system. Of course, they run out of budget. Supplier and customer are rolling over the floor: "your fault", "no, it your fault", etc. No one wants to defend the overrun to the higher level in the company.

Suddenly, some one suggests to take the costs for the parts of the system that will be used by other business units also, out of the original budget, and create an additional "pot of gold" for it. After all, it's not fair that this one BU pays all the costs on it's own. Applause. This is something they can defend to higher level. Their budget remains unchanged (with no overrun) and a new budget is created. The numbers remain the same, the fact that more money will be spend than originally thought remains unchanged, but this is fair and no one looses face. Yep, I was there. Was not my suggestion, sadly.

## Extra tasks

Imagine, in your project schedule you have planned "testing". Some stakeholders are highly committed to the deadlines for your schedule (they promised probably some one else). Your system will not be ready on this time for testing, at least not the entire system. You can propose to keep the deadline for "testing", and add an additional task after it called "integral testing" or "test it again, Sam". The stakeholders can remain their word (they just said "testing would be finished") and you have your extra time.

I am not claiming this works all the time. I'm just showing that you should be creative in the negotiation on budget and schedule.

# Chapter 6

## *Risk Management*

## 6.1. Dealing with the unknown

You have come a long way, all the way up to this chapter. I have discussed expectations, estimations and anticipations. I tried to make it sound as good as possible, but let's face it, it's all vague stuff. You have to think about how someone else thinks, and base your complete approach on that assessment. We handled requirements, and stated that it's best to assume that they are wrong and will change anyway. It's like flipping a coin or laying cards.

Software project management cannot be performed without a good practice to handle all these unknown parameters. A project manager has to be able to live with uncertainties, and have a good way to structure his approach to handle them. The first is a personal aspect, which you have to do all by yourself. The latter is where "risk management" comes in...

"*Risk management focuses the project manager's attention on those portions of the project most likely to cause trouble and to compromise participants' win conditions.*" [Boehm,1989 ]

So, in other words, it's a set of actions which helps the project manager structure his approach on dealing with the unknown or the "things not sure".

"*...we define risk as the possibility of loss. We obtain an instance of risk by specifying values for the risk attributes of probability (the possibility) and consequence (the loss). Probability is the likelihood that the consequence will occur. Consequence is the effect of an unsatisfactory outcome.*" [Hall, 1998]

So, the idea is to specify explicitly the items that you are not sure about and define what will happen if what is expected (or assumed) is not true.

If you are not sure about the estimate ending of a certain task, you can define the risk for this situation as follows: delay of the actual end of the activity * very likely to happen. What the consequences and advantages are of this approach, is the subject of this section.

### Risk is not a bad thing

The problem with risk management is the negative image of the word "risk". Of course, unless there is a potential for loss, there is no risk. The loss can be either a bad outcome or a lost opportunity. The tendency of most stakeholders is to jump very stressfully at the statement "this is a risk". Therefore most of the time it's not very easy to discuss about risks, because that's always a conversation about problems. It's very important the risk is not perceived as a bad thing, but as a positive attitude to make sure everyone will become a winner in the end.

Remember, risk management helps you being aware of the goals you have to achieve, and what can happen if you don't satisfy the goals. It supports you in making the right choices!

So, risk is not a bad thing! Say it loud! Spread the word!

## 6.2. Starting it all

What you don't know, can't hurt you.... You sure, right...not. When you are hooked on cigarettes, you smoke like a maniac, chances are you will claim you aren't addicted. Even if you can't stop, there's always this "if I really want, I can stop right away." You are in denial. You know you have a problem, but you're mentally not ready to accept it. In projects you also have these kind of "denial" things. You know problems can occur, but you just ignore them hoping they will blow over, will not happen anyway, you don't want to rock the boat, cross that bridge when we come to it...("...if there is a problem, we get over it...", lyrics of some old 80ties disco tune).

So, basically, there are things that you know you don't know. If you ignore them that's bad, but at least you know. And yep, there are more problematic things, the stuff you are not aware that you don't know them. They will sneak upon you, and you'll never know what hit you. It's very difficult to prepare yourself for the REALLY unknown.

If you have done this risk thing for years, you develop some nose for it. You have feelings ("FEELINGS, hohohoho, FEELINGS…lalala"), you have some gut stuff, etc. But how do you start this ability to identify risks? Or, how to bootstrap your gutt.

## Develop risk checklists

The answer my friend is…checklists. Start creating lists of points that you want to review for risks. As you do this more often, your checklist will grow, you can put all your experiences in it, in order to avoid having the problem in the future. But how to get started?

First of all, you are not alone. This is not a unique thing you are doing. So, of course, there are standard checklist you can start from. The Software Engineering Institute (www.sei.cmu.edu) provides a very nice starting point. The SEI risk taxonomy is a structured checklist that organises software development risks into a certain framework. But, with all the work you have done in the previous sections, you also come a long way. We could name it "Stakeholders Risk Taxonomy", or, more appropriately "the bloody list." I created it by writing down 30 minutes some aspects I covered in the previous chapters. It is not intended to be complete, it is merely intended as an example on how you can deduct checklist from this book.

## Stakeholders

- Have you identified all stakeholders?
- Have you identified from all groups the leader or spokesman?
- Have you ever met the stakeholders?
- Do you have information on the background of the stakeholders (history)?

## Stakes

*Fears*

- Do you know what the fears are generally for the type of stakeholders you have (e.g. programmers)?
- Do you know what the fears are of the stakeholders per group?
- Do you know what the fears are for each individual?
- Do you know how this project affects the fears of the stakeholders?

*Wishes*

- Do you know what the wishes are generally for the type of stakeholders you have (e.g. programmers)?
- Do you know what the wishes are of the stakeholders per group?
- Do you know what the wishes are for each individual?
- Do you know how this project affects the wishes of the stakeholders?

## Requirements

*Product*

- Are the cause and goal of the project clear to you?
- Is the project scope identified and does it include what you can change, what you must change, and what you can't change?

*Process*

- Are the constraints identified (money, time, people)?
- Do you have any idea how much room there is to negotiate these constraints?
- If there are already estimations, do you know how much you can trust them?
- Is the project strategy clear and easy?
- Is the project organisation identified? Does every member have added value to the project?

### Project management

- Are you able to negotiate?
- Are you able to think in win-win situations?
- Are you risk averse?
- Do you include your own stakes into the process?
- Are you able to give the project back in case it smells like a trap?

### Feedback

- Is everyone aware for the need and use of giving feedback?
- Have you any idea how to provide feedback?
- Do you really understand the techniques you want to use?
- Did you schedule (time, money, people) activities to provide the feedback?

## 6.3. Writing it down

In the previous section we talked about how to start talking about the risks. You take a certain aspect and think about it in terms of what you don't know or what might go different then expected. Even better, you do this exercise with some colleagues in a meeting. For every risk that you might come up, you have to specify the following items:

- *Risk*; A description of the actual risk. Example: Uncertainty availability programming resources.
- *Impact* (or consequence); The impact on the project (process or product) if the risk occurs. Example: Delay in construction interfaces.
- *Possibility*; The possibility that the risk occurs (use e.g. high/medium/low). Example: Medium
- *Action*; The action that can/will be taken to avoid the risk from happening or reduce the chance for it, or reduce the impact. Example: Get planning clear. Investigate possibility external programmers.

- *Cost*; What is the cost if the risk occurs (time and money). Example: Delay 3 weeks.

You have to review the list that is generated in this way periodically (once a week). If the list is too large to give all the risks your attention, you have to create some priorities. A nice way is to create every time a top ten of the most urgent risks, so you will be sure you focus on the more important ones.

There are a lot more things to say about the subject of risk management. But first of all it's a state of mind. And with the few things shown in the section, you have a good starting point to reach the state. Remember, risk is not a bad thing, and if you come up with an action to resolve it, execute it…don't just talk the talk, but walk the risk management.

# Chapter 7

## *The Bigger Picture*

## 7.1. No project is an island

Every zoo tries to get a very nice and balanced variety of animals to present to its visitors. Species are grouped together, in a coherent way, and if you follow the tour that's laid out for you, you flow through nature in a natural way. But there is always this small pavilion at the back of the wall, in the shadows of the trees, where they keep the ugly and weird animals. They must be in the zoo for completeness, but they never fit anywhere in the normal tour. If you insert them anywhere, they interrupt the flow.

My last chapter is the pavilion in the back of the book. It tells two stories that have to be told, but only fit at the end of the text, on their own. They tell the stories of doing the projects within your *organisation*. Your organisation is not a person, it's a collection of people, but even this non-human institute has stakes and requirements. They are called *policies*. The first story is about handling policies issued on what software you may make or buy.

The second member of the pavilion is the introduction of a project style of working within your organisation. It's nice if in the end you know as a project manager what to do, but if more people within your organisation are in tune with how software projects should be done, it would increase your effectiveness significantly. However, traditionally this is done from the top down, as a directive from above. And this is the most fundamental mistake you can make.

## 7.2. Handling Policies

Why does the chicken cross the road? To get to the other side. Now a little more difficult.... Why do the English drive at the left side of the road? Personally I have no idea where this "left side" comes from, and, personally, I don't care. These Islanders just made an agreement once, and stuck to it, just to avoid running into each other.

Why does the software I want to buy for the company has to comply with J2EE standards, ISO standards, etc? First of all, I don't know what they mean, and second...why? If you go out eating, you don't care if they use a Siemens or a Philips microwave to nuke the food. However, you do want to keep your stomach at ease.

At companies, large and small, there will be some statements made about what your software should look like, and to which specifics it must comply. The Policies. They're annoying, they're anonymous and they're here to stay. "All information systems should have a 3-tier architecture." This is what a typical policy looks like. In case you will stumble across one, you will recognise the beast. It actually sounds like a requirement, doesn't it? No wonder, it actually is.

## Policies are requirements too

Policies can be viewed as requirements made by the company itself. Following the argument of this book, the company should have stakes. I know, I argued in chapter "Intake" that only individuals have stakes, as it is a person who has fears and wishes. At the end of it all, I'm not taking that back. With company stakes it's only difficult to pinpoint exactly its original owner. Can be the board of directors, your boss or the "Policy Department" (those guys walking in toga's and stating the obvious as Nobel prize winning stuff). It also may be stakes that are inherent to operating a company, like "making a profit", so "we should earn more than we spend."

Back to the original question, why does the software I want to buy (or perhaps make) have to comply with certain policies? For the same reason it has to satisfy the stakes of the stakeholders; to make everyone a winner (including the company), so you have a happy and successful project. If the policies are the requirements, what are the stakes and can you change the policies? Now, that's worth some thinking.

Consider the situation where a toga from the Policy Department descends from his ivory tower to the mud of the software project. He has with him a paper role which content he shares with you in a loud voice: "Hear, fools, hear. Thou shall comply to these standards: J2EE, ISO and OSI. Thou shall use these techniques: UML, DPL and JBF." The crowd goes wild, sets fire to his paper role and kicks him back up into the tower. However, his glass tower is next to the quarters of Zeus, the Almighty Boss, who hears the whining of the toga and sends his thunder upon your little project. Thou shall comply.

You can ignore it, but you will get trampled upon. You can fully comply, and you have stuff that no one wants, no one with money to pay for it at least. So, you have to dive into the stakes that are behind the policies. And most of the time they are good ones, things that really benefit your project, and your company and, in the end, you.

## Thou shall use The Big O

What are the stakes? I cannot be specific, there can be a lot of things. But perhaps some examples I experienced may help you on your way. "Every database should be Oracle." (or just pick a vendor you like). When buying a system, it can be simple. "Does it run Oracle? No? Sorry, we don't want it." But, normally you buy functionality and not technology. You buy a system for what it can do, and not because the bits and bytes are flipped in a certain way. For normal use, you buy a car to get you from point A to point B, and not because it has yellow spark plugs. You can ask the supplier to port its system to the desired database vendor, but you get a special version of the system (which is a nightmare in maintenance) and likely the supplier has limited knowledge about this particular database.

The stake here has to do with sharing database administrators among several systems. The company benefits from efficient use of employees. Especially concerning specialised people. Database administrators

(DBAs) are a good example. Having more similar systems that these people can maintain, will make the costs of maintenance drop. Using a more mainstream database like Oracle, makes it also easier to get some outside people from the market to do the tasks when your own employees are overloaded or not available.

In this case it is not that the database should be Oracle, but that we should make efficient use of the current DBAs, and should have no problem finding outside people to handle the system. Now, that's a company stake!

## What language?

Someone told me once: "If it ain't programmed in Java following the Extreme Programming principles, we don't want to buy the software." Arguing about why he put this statement so firmly, the person orated for an hour on the great advantages Java has in respect to more traditional programming languages. And in combination with principles from Extreme Programming the resulting software would be perfect. He was talking about policies put onto a system he was going to buy…

Do you care in what language your word processor is written? Delphi, Smalltalk, C++ or Miranda? Probably you don't. Why should you care then when it's a specific information system you buy? You should pay attention to this aspect, that's for sure. But, not because the syntax is so neat, and certainly not because some external bureau, (or a Guru on a seminar) has yelled that Java is the way to go.

So, why should you consider these aspects? For the use of the software itself you don't care what is under the hood; if it runs, it runs. But for the continuation of the system in the future it is a factor to consider. If an obscure programming language is used, it may be difficult in the future to find good programmers skilled in this particular language. This is definitely a risk for the quality of the software in the long run; as you know, people come and people go, also programmers. As for programming principles, let everyone program in on the way that works for them best. Just look for principles; are they available and used? The companies only stake is to have no surprises, in the quality of the software and in the process of constructing the software.

Like before, with the stakes you can do something. They're valid business arguments and leave some room to operate. Still wonder what the stakes were of the guy that told me "if it ain't programmed..."? I guess he has programmers employed, who want to program using way cool techniques they have learned at a seminar. But that's just my guess.

## Are you thin?

Software architectural discussion are always the best. You draw four boxes with several arrows between them, and state that all systems should comply with this architectural design. "All systems should use a 3-tier architecture". I will not explain what it is (if you want to know, just look it up), only that in the segment where I operate there are *very* few systems that follow this architecture (at the moment I write this book). So, you have to build it yourself?

Searching for the stakes took my quite some time. Talking to toga's, dissecting there arguments, turning them over, looking up close, looking from far with my eyes almost shut.... The effect of this policy is that on workstations less software is installed then traditional, the so called thin-clients, which seems to be easier to maintain. Second effect seems to be less network traffic, which allows the purchase of less bandwidth and saving money.

Ease of maintenance and saving money on bandwidth are in the end the original stakes of the company. Die hard technicians might now complain: "that's not the real power of 3-tier". Perhaps they're right. The point is, it doesn't matter. The requirement is formulated, correct or incorrect, but it's the stake that's important. So before redesigning your system you can consider cheaper alternatives for saving bandwidth and ease of maintenance. You go against the policies. But presenting the alternative requirements in such a fashion they keep supporting the stakes, is most of the time a winner. It is at least worth a discussion.

## Respecting the unborn child

When buying a house, some of my friends want extra room for the kids, they might get, someday, maybe. They try to anticipate the coming of the unborn, better yet, the unconceived child. While purchasing a house this kind of anticipation is easy, one child is one room extra. You do the calculations.

Consider the following situation: the current system is in state of collapse, there is a technical necessity to replace the software. That's the cause and goal of a little happy project. Parallel to it are some larger projects, that are "strategic", and therefor have larger visibility and in perception a higher priority. Policy is you have to consider the "strategic" projects and keep in line with them. As you know "strategic" means large time frames, vague requirements, and big changes, sorry, reorientation. Try to keep in line with stuff that can't give you a date, or specific requirements, let alone, the quantified benefits. It's like saying to a professional athlete to keep in the same pace of this senior citizen with a Zimmer-frame. What do you mean, slowing down?

Again, the story becomes annoying, you should focus on the cause and goal of "strategic" projects, they can be considered as stakes. Try to create the situation where you can align with the projects when they have things clear. Try to avoid the situations where you make it impossible to align anyway. Don't say, forget it; "strategic" means a lot of higher people are watching, and giving the finger to higher management is always a bad career move.

## 7.3. Introducing projects in the organisation

Until now it was all about what *you* could do as a project manager; the approach was self-centred, like a self help book: "How to get rich in a millisecond." You will come a long way on your own, but you will never reach the full potential, the fullest effect you can reach with this kind of negotiating style of software project management. This section will provide some insight in how to introduce some "elements" of projects into an organisation and its employees.

Don't think when your organisation is already accustomed to doing projects, this section is not relevant for you. Surely, the "official way" of performing the projects is not in line with "The Flow of Stakes" (see chapter 1), and new people will always be added to the organisation.

### Not invented here

Do you know the best way to frustrate a perfectly good process? Give a directive. Tell the employees they have to work in a certain way. Tell them they must. You will see your oiled machinery get sabotaged and run into a definite hold. People are funny in this respect, if it concerns their own work, they want something to say about it. They want to determine how they work. When introducing a project style of working into an organisation this is one of the main causes for failure.

Some years ago I experienced an organisation where all projects were torpedoed by changing requirements. In a need to get a grip on the situation the project managers looked for techniques to control the situation. They found out they had it all, they installed already every procedure that they could find in literature. And still, the projects were sinking under the heavy burden of continuos change. By accident they stumbled across a project team member at the coffee machine claiming that "the procedure was installed, but no one was actually using it. The project manager issued this procedure out of the blue, so, it's his darn thing. Not mine."

This phenomenon has actually a name: the not-invented-here syndrome. Not accepting something because it's not yours. It's around you, more then you can imagine. Why am I telling you this at this moment? Because a lot of introductions on doing projects are directives from above: "starting next month you will have to make a plan for every work you do; you have to record all the time you spend on tasks." And like I started out this section, that is a good way to frustrate a process.

Next to this "acceptance" issue is another argument to let the people involved determine the way thy shall work...who knows better how to work, then the people performing the job?

If giving a directive is not a good way to introduce it, what will be the alternative for the top down approach? Well.... How about bottom up?

## Bottom up: knowing what you do

Raising a child has its problems. You can tell 42 times "don't run, you might fall", but actually having a little (innocent!) fall makes a more lasting impression. This doesn't mean that the parent is better off throwing the kid on the pavement. The parent tries to guide the child as good as it is able to, through the process of learning and experiencing. And this wisdom from someone who hasn't kids.

Back to the kids in the organisation. Starting the "new way of working" at the individual employee level raises the critique that the employees are too stupid to change. "They perform this job in this way for 30-years. These guys are too old to change." And more arguments like this one. Instructing employees to deliver you a process description that complies to a project-approach doesn't work. I agree. But a little guidance in the activity creates miracles.

The guidance should consist of answering the big 'why': why do we need a new process? Why should it look like this? You could provide everyone this fabulous book. People should know why the game is played like this, that's the key to success.

To middle management who will get the role of customer 'visibility' should be the mantra. Schedules, budgets and results will be transparent. Issues will be made clear by the project manager, to avoid as much surprises as possible. That will probably sell itself. Some discipline from the customer is of course required. Ambitious goals with no budget and a very narrow timeframe will be killed from the start. The only thing made transparent is its impossibility. The visibility also makes it difficult to change your mind. Middle management can change their initial thoughts, but it's 100% clear minds are changed; it's impossible to claim you are saying the same thing as you always did. This can be a drawback for managers.

For technical employees, like programmers, the trick is to show them "better planning, is more relaxed". If for example programmers can provide the project manager with a perfect estimate on how long they need for a certain job, they can do their work in their own pace, without time schedules slipping and pressure building. Assuming the project manager doesn't slash every estimate by 50%. When this is clear, just show them the way to improve their ability to plan. Watts Humphrey [1995] has constructed a complete process for this. The essence is to let people record what they are doing, and how long it takes. They can see for themselves which tasks consume most time, so they can take action to improve them. It makes visible how long a certain tasks actually takes. When asked for an estimate they can make a more informed guess, based upon their records on previous tasks. "System X cost me 1 month. This one has a little more functionality, so I would estimate for this system 2 months."

So, filling out timesheets is the way to go? Not if you put it like that. Just read the previous paragraph again and compare it with using timesheets to control the programmers in a directive manner: "You are late! Why?", "This takes too long! Why?" You will be heading for a disaster.

## Top down: best practices

Having all those individual employees improving themselves is not enough. First of all, from the top down incentives must be provided to keep the people going. It is after all extra workload, so someone should better appreciate it.

Finally, let someone in the organisation collect all the lessons learned from the individuals, and summarise it as an integrated and coherent set of best practices. For this purpose, best practices are always better then a complete method, as the best practices are really invented here!

# Epilogue

*The Microwave Way to Software Project Management* takes you on a fast, entertaining and essential tour through the jungle software project managers can and will walk in to. The ride starts at the mindset of the project manager; he should have one simple mental image of the jobs he has to perform, instead of trying to stuff 500 pages of charting and calculating in his head. He should know the flow of stakes.

For a lot of readers one conclusion still comes as a big surprise: doing projects is a peoples business. It's all about keeping everyone involved in the project happy by supporting their stakes. The trouble with stakes is, no one tells you what they are. You have to guess, negotiate, anticipate and manipulate to get past the requirements directly through to the fears and wishes of people. Software project management is more about psychology than technology.

This book presents how in the real world of enterprises the 'traditional' techniques of project management, like Gantt-charting, can be used as communications techniques to keep some persons happy. *The Microwave Way* is not about knowing you have a deadline, but about how to move it. Naming a date is easy, telling you cannot make it, is the real job.

Having fun, and doing it fast. That's the intention of this pocket-book. Helping you to be the best software project manager you can be, while having fun and doing this fast. The Microwave Way. However, this is not an instant way to success. It's not a pill you can take and all the troubles are gone. It's a state of mind, a way of living. It will take commitment and discipline to put into action, to get the real benefit out of it. The transfer of knowledge is fast and fun, but it will take a long time to digest all you consumed. So, it really is the Microwave Way, in every aspect.

# epilogue

# About the Author

Bas de Baar works as a project manager within the publishing industry. He holds a degree in Business Informatics and lives currently with his wife in Zandvoort, The Netherlands.

# References

[Boehm, 1989] "Theory-W Software Project Management: Principles and Examples" Barry W. Boehm and Rony Ross, IEEE Transactions on Software Engineering, Vol. 15, No. 7, July 1989.

[Brooks, 1995] "The mythical man-month, essays on software engineering", anniversary edition, Frederick P. Brooks, 1995, Addison-Wesley.

[Hall, 1998] "Managing risk, methods for software system development", Elaine M. Hall, 1998, Addison-Wesley, SEI Series in Software Engineering.

[D'Herbemont and Cesar, 1998] "Managing sensitive projects, a lateral approach", Olivier D'Herbemont and Bruno Cesar, 1998, MacMillan Press.

[Humphrey, 1989] "Managing the Software Process", Watts S. Humphrey, 1989, Addison-Wesley Publishing.

[Humphrey, 1995] "A Discipline for Software Engineering", Watts S. Humphrey, 1995, Addison-Wesley Publishing.

[Fisher and Ury, 1983] "Getting to yes, negotiating agreement without giving in", Roger Fisher and William Ury, 1983, Penguin Books.

[Gray, 1992] "Man are from Mars, women are from Venus", John Gray, 1992, HarperTrade.

[Hoff, 1982] "The Tao of Pooh", Benjamin Hoff, 1982, Penguin Books.

[Martin, 1991] "Rapid Application Development", James Martin, 1991, MacMillan Publishing Company.

# Index

0-595-22711-2

www.ingramcontent.com/pod-product-compliance
Lightning Source LLC
Chambersburg PA
CBHW021146070326
40689CB00044B/1151

* 9 7 8 0 5 9 5 2 2 7 1 1 2 *